THE FORAGER'S
Kitchen Handbook

THE FORAGER'S
Kitchen Handbook

**FORAGING TIPS AND OVER 100 RECIPES
USING WHAT YOU CAN FIND FOR FREE**

Fiona Bird

CICO BOOKS
LONDON NEW YORK

This book is for everyone who loves rainbows and strives to cook with ingredients that are both local and in season.

This edition published in 2021 by CICO Books
An imprint of Ryland Peters & Small Ltd
341 E 116th St, New York NY 10012
20–21 Jockey's Fields, London WC1R 4BW

www.rylandpeters.com

10 9 8 7 6 5 4 3 2

First published in 2013 as *The Forager's Kitchen*

Text © Fiona Bird 2013, 2021
Design and photography © CICO Books 2013

A CIP catalog record for this book is available from the Library of Congress and the British Library.

ISBN 978 1 78249 876 6

Printed in China

Copy Editor: Lee Faber
Designer: Alison Fenton
Photography: Peter Moore (foraging photos), Stuart West (recipe photos), plus see page 192 for additional credits
Home Economist: Louise Wagstaffe
Food Stylist: Luis Peral Aranda

The author and publisher add a word of caution: Foraging wild ingredients requires expert knowledge and identification. They cannot be held responsible for, or shall not be liable for, the erroneous consumption of wild plants that have caused severe or allergic reactions resulting from misidentification. The photographs and text in this book should not be used alone for identification purposes.

MIX
Paper from
responsible sources
FSC® C008047

contents

Introduction

The foraging cook brings the tastes and scents of the countryside to the kitchen table, wherever that table may be. I divide my time between the stunning glens of rural Angus and the Outer Hebridean Isle of South Uist, where my husband is the island doctor. As a mother of six who enjoys foraging and cooking, my local food supplies vary from Angus hedgerow, moors, and woodland to Hebridean coast, "machair" (fertile, low-lying grassy plain found on the coastlines of north-west Ireland and Scotland), peatland, and lakeside. In season, there is an abundance of seaweed, bog myrtle, sweet cicely, and meadowsweet. I am a fortunate woman.

Foraging takes time, and Scottish weather is often mixed, but with some gently cajoled help from our family and friends, it has become a perfect recipe for outdoor teamwork. With luck and a bit of effort, supper can be "off the land," in other words, "free, not bought." I describe my foraging expeditions as capers, and yes, I collect prolific budded flowers too, but even a tenacious forager can return home with an empty basket. Favorite gathering spots may have been overpicked, or in some

years a particular ingredient's season is paltry. Even the most tenacious forager is accepting of a fruitless expedition. Take a lighthearted approach, and enjoy the foraging journey as much as the gathering experience. A little wayside nibbling or "wild grazing" en route home, is, of course, a forager's pleasure.

I have a great affection for rural Scotland, but foraging here may require a wetsuit and pair of not just thorn-proof, but fleeced-for-warmth, gloves. City dwellers may be able to forage with less exposure to the elements as our eldest son, Xander, our stalwart elderflower cordial maker, has found. Inspired by a pink elderflower bush in his grandmother's garden, he now hunts pink elderflowers on London wasteland. In elderflower season, Xander is synonymous with not only a very sticky kitchen, but also a tiny corner of a freezer tightly packed with bottles full of elderflower cordial. Kitchens may be cleaned throughout the year, but the elderflower season passes all too quickly. Seize the season before it, like the faded bloom or withered berry, has disappeared, leaving the tardy foraging cook with a long year of waiting. However, as the seasons move on, so the foraging family memories and knowledge pass down the generations, cementing longlasting family and food connections.

Many basic ingredients can be frozen, but to my mind this does little for the freshness or for the spirit of foraging, and encourages greed. Foraging is more about enjoying the moment than saving for a rainy day. Even so, I have noticed that when foraging, the berry or blossom a wee bit further away always looks more tempting. Indeed, the grass may be greener over the fence, or hedge, but try to be content with a basket of what is just enough for today. The foraging cook

ABOVE LEFT: *The urban forager can often be rewarded with a fine harvest of blackberries.*
OPPOSITE: *A springtime carpet of wild garlic (also known as ramps or ramsons).*

ABOVE: *One of my local beaches yields a fine crop of mussels.*

learning to ride a bicycle (a forager needs one with a basket), it becomes easier with the passing of time. Forage as you would cycle: safely, mindful of others, with respect for the laws of the land, and with one final maxim: "if in doubt, leave it out."

A foraging cook will learn to know how much sugar to add to blossom syrup, and when a flower has enough coats of egg wash, or syrup to crystallize. For some things there is a wee bit of trial and error. With growing confidence, you may prefer to make a more concentrated syrup than for a traditional cordial, and then dilute it further on use. It will certainly take up less storage space.

Most of my recipes use small jars and bottles and when the season is past, I simply move on to the next ingredient. Hedgerow jam tastes better on a warm summer morning than in dark, frosty winter.

I could so easily gather everything for my own pot, but I also enjoy watching the common blue butterfly (a dull choice of name for such a beautiful creation), striking dragonfly, buzzing bee, and birds that need to snack too; foraging is about sharing. If I overindulge, a future generation may not be able to enjoy the simple foraging pleasure that we have shared as a family. As a child, I remember picking cowslips with my father and sister for my mother and grandmothers; today, cowslips are a protected species and we can only dream of cowslip wine, cake, or curd. We have a duty to act as responsible custodians of the land. Every individual deserves the opportunity to forage.

Equipped with didactic knowledge (perhaps from a foraging course), we can all harvest ingredients from a rich and diverse natural food supply, and have little need for commercially foraged products. As confidence grows, the thrifty, careful forager will enjoy food without payment, while ensuring that today's free food leaves plenty for tomorrow.

FIONA BIRD

should be, by nature, a seasonal cook; the provenance —its place of origin—is guaranteed.

Over the years, I've learnt that the maxim "small is beautiful" is definitely good for the forager. On a practical level, 1 pint (600ml) cordial bottles defrost quickly if frozen and have less time to deteriorate on the fridge shelf. Less really is more: filling bottles or jars ad infinitum can become dull. Just a few handfuls of a foraged ingredient concentrate the attention more than armfuls, and cooking becomes more imaginative. Foraging to fill your pantry or store cupboard takes a long time, is a bit greedy, and raises the question of sustainability. So forage for your own pot, and not the neighborhood's.

Intensive farming, with its associated destruction of hedgerows by machinery, is distressing, not just because my basket takes longer to fill, but because the birds and the bees are losers too.

There are rules of the countryside to adhere to, and weathers to tolerate, but tenacity is the key, and like

Ground Rules

Each recipe in this collection focuses on a particular wild edible, which, with a bit of luck, will result in a greater appreciation and understanding of wild ingredients. Hopefully, this will not only lead to an increased desire to forage, but will also establish rudimentary building blocks that associate the food we eat with its natural habitat. If we are aware of the wild foods that grow where deer feed, flavors such as wild thyme, blackberries, juniper, bilberries, and rowan berries will be the foraging cook's natural venison choice.

The countryside is there for each and every one of us, and foraging courses can help to give the less knowledgeable an awareness that can be traced back to our forebear hunter gatherers. There are, however, national and local rules to understand. As a rule of thumb: forage only where ingredients are plentiful, and for your own pot, not that of the neighborhood. Never take more than one-sixth of anything, and roots should not be removed without the permission of the landowner. This book does not contain any recipes using roots. DON'T SPADE OR FORK IT.

Commercial foragers require special licenses to go about their business. Sadly, in my mind, this removes one of the most satisfying elements of foraging—the sheer exhilaration of searching and finding. This is the harvester's simplest pleasure. It can't be packaged, no matter how authentic the wild artisan producer's pot or bottle. The contents may be wild, but the experience can't be bottled.

A little foraging excitement goes a long way, and foragers need to learn to be happiest when their basket is half-full rather than half-empty.

Misidentification

This can be a very serious issue but my suggestion is never to cook with an ingredient, unless you are 100% sure that you know what it is.

IF IN DOUBT, LEAVE IT OUT.

Take a pocket guide into the countryside, but after picking, "reference match" at home with a comprehensive book (the type that is too heavy to go in a rucksack). Do this at least twice before cooking with an ingredient if you have the slightest identification doubt. Alternatively, go with a friend with "wild know-how" and your friend will tell you what you can, or can't, do.

The elderly, pregnant, nursing mothers, and those with allergies, should be particularly careful when foraging. Today, there is a tendency to be over-anxious about sell-by dates on food, and this is often transferred to an inbuilt fear of the consumption of wild foods, shellfish and mushrooms in particular.

I fully appreciate this but, as a mother of six, I have at various times been obliged to tolerate a little more dirt in my kitchen than the average mother of two. Suffice it to say, my children have lived to tell the tale. As a family, we have eaten shellfish out of season and numerous wild mushrooms with no ill effect. However, I cannot stress the importance of foraging with somebody in the foraging know; hopefully, I fit this bill.

When to forage

For everything there is a season; try to forage for the moment, not for tomorrow. Freezers can be filled year in, year out from a visit to the supermarket. Try not to be greedy, and squirrel the bounty of a summer harvest to gather freezer burn, and possible "garbage can (dustbin) sacrifice" at Christmas. Freezing may extend the season, but I'm not sure that it enhances taste. It certainly tempts a greedy forager.

How to forage

Obey the rules of the countryside: Close gates, control dogs, and if a sign says "keep out," do exactly that. Foraging should be a relaxing, fulfilling pastime, concentrating on the beauty and natural pantry (larder) of the countryside, not a battle of establishing common rights. National and local laws and quotas must be respected (see pages 9 and 188–189).

Avoid roots and forage small amounts of the FOUR Fs: flowers, fungi, fruits, and foliage. Look for seaweed and shellfish, too, but only for your kitchen table. The fresh air that we breathe is like the food the forager gathers, "freely available." Nobody should have to survive on a diet of processed food. The forager is indeed a fortunate person, and one who is not easily and conveniently satisfied.

Where to forage

Forage in dog-free woods when possible, and in cities and towns, gather above the level where animals relieve themselves. Avoid areas close to crops that have been sprayed with insecticides, or roadside shoulders (verges) where car fumes can penetrate.

Forage only on clean beaches and in rivers and streams where the water is fast moving, and keep a careful eye on tides and the weather. Do not forage in public parks.

ABOVE: *Hawthorn in full bloom*

Ground Rules

Useful Kit for Foragers

This list is not extensive, and some of the kitchen equipment is expensive. A food dehydrator is really useful for foragers; seaweed dries quickly and fruit leathers dry evenly. Wild sorbets and ice creams are unique, and an ice-cream maker produces much smoother results than if you make them by hand.

Kitchen Equipment

* Heavy-duty stand mixer
* Food dehydrator: for drying fruit leathers, leaves, berries, seaweeds
* Juice extractor: for juicing, and also for leaves e.g. ramps (wild garlic) for oil
* Deep fat fryer for tempura
* Food processor for seaweed, fruit, and herb purées
* Coffee grinder for seaweeds and leaves for tisanes
* Jelly bag and strainer
* Preserving pan and thermometer
* Stainless steel straining funnel
* Large strainer/sieve
* Colander
* Jam-jar funnel
* Small preserving bottles for cordials
* Cheesecloth (muslin) squares
* Large beaded food covers for buckets of steeping cordial/flower blossoms
* Small preserving jam jars, lids, and labels
* Silicone ice-cube trays for herbs and purées
* Digital scales for weighing delicate blossoms
* Steam juicer

Foraging Kit

* Rake for clamming (cockling)
* Sturdy scissors
* Small knife
* Small rolls of plastic bags and bag ties
* Small basket for mushrooms and leaves
* Antiseptic wipes and band-aids (plasters)
* Salt, for razor clams
* Small lightweight bucket with a handle for shellfish
* Plastic grocery (carrier) bags for seaweeds and blossoms
* Damp cloth to prevent plants drying out

Clothing

Living in Scotland I have to say there is no such thing as poor weather, just badly clothed foragers.

* Waterproof jacket and trousers
* Wetsuit for collecting seaweeds
* Wellington (rain) boots (can be slippery on rocks, but these are useful in the countryside)
* Non-slip waterproof shoes
* Gloves
* Small towel
* Small backpack
* Cellphone (mobile phone) and whistle for safety

CHAPTER 1

FLOWERS *and* *Blossom*

Edible Flowers

I had to make searching choices here. The recipes use small quantities —flowers are beautiful, so leave plenty for others to appreciate, and be guided by your nose. Wean friends into your scented kitchen gently, and change your scent with the season.

Edible Flowers

Angelica
Bitter vetch
Blackthorn
Blackberry blossom
Borage
Chickweed
Clover
Daisy (for my taste, in moderation)
Dandelions
Dog rose
Elderflower
Garlic mustard
Hawthorn (May blossom)
Honeysuckle (but not the berries)
Lady's smock (cuckoo flower)
Lilac
Linden (lime) blossom
Mallow
Meadowsweet
Mint
Primrose
Ramps (wild garlic)
Rosa rugosa
Sweet cicely
Violets
Watercress
White dead nettle
Wild cherry blossom
Wild thyme
Wild strawberries

This list is far from extensive, but mentions some of the flowers that I have used in the recipes in this book. It doesn't included any protected flowers, such as cowslip, which you will find in old cookery books.

ABOVE FROM TOP: *Dandelion; dog rose (*Rosa canina)*; wild strawberry.*

Poisonous Flowers

Buttercup   Foxglove   Hemlock

Do not be tempted by these common flowers; again the list is not comprehensive. Always check with a handbook before you eat any flower, leaf, or berry.

Consult a poisonous plant book or website to familiarize yourself with harmful species, and when foraging for *Meadow Flower Scented Honey*, page 48, do not be tempted to pick buttercups, as they are poisonous (although very pretty.) With regard to folklore, scientists say that the yellow glow you get when holding a buttercup under your chin has nothing to do with liking butter. It is mainly due to the epidermal layer of the petal reflecting yellow light.

I've listed hemlock because it can be confused with angelica and sweet cicely. If you can recognize hemlock, you will know it as a plant to give a foraging miss.

Foxglove—I mention this because the foxglove, which has life-saving properties (digitalis is used as a medication for some heart patients) is very toxic, and fatal with an overdose, so its potency must be measured very carefully. It should NOT be eaten.

NEVER use inedible flowers for decoration purposes.

Wild flowers and herbs

I have sourced much of the inspiration for my wildflower recipes from researching the recipes of Hannah Glasse, *The Gentle Art of Cookery* by Mrs C. F. Leyel and Miss Olga Hartley, and Mrs Beeton.

✓ Harvest after the dew has dried, and before the intense heat of the sun (with the exception of blossoms for cordials and syrups).
✓ Shake the flowers well after picking to leave any insects in local surroundings.
✓ Remove pistil and stamens (usually green): they taste bitter.
✓ Avoid washing flowers, if at all possible. Shake and brush dirt off with a pastry brush, or use a fine water plant spray.

✓ Flowers can be stored in a refrigerator for a week. I traveled from Scotland to Birmingham (350 miles), and my flowers arrived in perfect condition after having been packed in a child's lunch box with an ice pack. Flowers will also freeze well.
✓ Always check in a reference book to ensure that a flower is edible unless you are 100% certain. If in DOUBT, leave it OUT.
✗ Avoid plants that may have been sprayed with pesticides, or exposed to carbon monoxide or animal excretions.
✗ Do not pick protected species, or where blooms are sparse.
✗ If you have any allergies, consult your doctor before eating flowers.

Flower and herb sugars and salts

It is difficult to give exact quantities for flower and herb sugars and salts because flavors differ. Wild mint, sweet cicely, and thyme will scent sugar or salt with greater ease than, say, dog rose petals. I have tried various ways of making flower and herb sugars and salts: drying them and mixing with sugar or salt in a food processor or laying the dry petals or leaves in a jam jar with superfine (caster) sugar or salt. DRY is the key word here, and SHAKE the sealed jar WELL periodically. If you simply stuff foraged flowers into a jar with sugar and pop a lid on, the result will be one sticky mess. I had some success (when rushed) when I layered ramps (wild garlic) flowers with salt in a tiny jar without a lid on a sunny windowsill. I then blitzed the rather lumpy salt in a food processor. Use the sugars and salts as soon as you can.

CRYSTALLIZED *Flowers*

The textbook will suggest that you can either use egg white and sugar or gum arabic, which in my rural-living experience is tricky to come by. The egg wash idea is simple: I've experimented with gin and violets, and so by natural progression, put some gin in with the egg white, but you could use any clear alcohol. Use an unrefined sugar, and be prepared to practice on the first batch.

Makes about ⅓ cup (75ml)

What to forage and find:
* 1 egg white, lightly whisked
* ½ teaspoon gin (aids drying)
* Wild flowers or petals
* ½ cup (100g) unrefined superfine (caster) sugar

What to do:

1 Paint the lightly whisked egg white and gin onto the flower petals.

2 Use your fingers to scatter sugar over the flower/petal, then put it on a sheet of parchment paper on a sunny windowsill to dry. Tweezers are useful for picking up delicate, crystallized petals and flowers.

3 Once dried, store in an airtight tin and use as soon as possible.

Wild Notes

You can also crystallize leaves and flowers using flower syrups (see Sweet Cicely Syrup, page 130.) I have used confectioners' (icing) sugar as well as superfine (caster); the superfine gives a smoother effect. Confectioners' sugar tends to dry in clogged lumps.

About Elder

Sambucus nigra

"Hawthorn blooms and Elder flowers
fill a house will evil powers"
Herbal Magick, Gerina Dunwich

Colloquial names:
*Common Elder, Devil's Wood, Judas Tree
Scaven, Whit Aller, Bore Tree, Black-Berried
Elder, Boon Tree, Sweet Elder, Fairy Tree, Dog
Tree, Devil's Eye, ElderBlow, Blueberry Elder*

Where to find:
In hedgerows and woods, and on scrub or
wasteland, but a sensible person will not
disturb a bush that has become a garden
settler. The elder roots with ease, and grows
with speed. It has been described as a typical
product of contemporary life: an opportunist
that is easily grown and replaced. There is a
private graveyard beyond our garden wall
which, in season, is a mass of elderflower
blossoms, so we are well supplied, but we
have to forge a path through stinging
nettles—gatherers don boots (the stinging
nettles have died back by elderberry season).

The elder is a member of the honeysuckle
family and is bigger than a bush, but makes a
spindly tree. In late spring and early summer,
the 2–2½-inch (5–6cm) umbrella clusters of
tiny, creamy, lace-like flowers fill the air with
a distinctive smell, which reminds me of
honey. After the flowers comes a fall treat—
bunches of Lilliputian-sized black berries,
which hang heavily from the tree. Trees vary
in size and, if you are lucky, you may spy
Black Beauty or Black Lace (*Sambucas nigra*),
a pink-flowering species with black leaves. Its
blossom can be used to make bubble-gum-
pink cordial or elderflower champagne.

How to forage and gather:
Elderflowers: Pick the cream flowers in early
summer in midday sunshine (never in rain),
when they are fully open. Avoid any

blossoms with a hint
of brown. Cut the
stems by hand or use
scissors. Collect
blossoms in a
basket—the fragile
flowers may crush in
a plastic bag. Shake
blossoms well to remove visiting guests,
but do not wash them or you will lose the
heady, floral fragrance. Don't be overly
greedy or there won't be any berries to
forage in the fall, and don't pick blossom
that is leaving a trail on the ground; it will
be past its sell-by date.

Elderberries: Gather in fall, but wait until
the berries are the deepest wine red, almost
black. Carefully break the umbrella-shaped
berry clusters from the stems. Take a stick to
help lower higher branches. Leave some for
birds—they are on berry watch, too. Harvest
well before they start to shrivel and dry.

How to use:
Elderflowers: Use in cordials, wines, infused
in tisanes, vinegars, sorbets, ice creams,
jams, crumbles, and custards. The flower
head is yummy, if not healthy, deep-fried in
a sweetened batter. Elderflowers have an
affinity with gooseberries and strawberries.
In my mind, the flowers herald the start of
summer, and work well when infused with
early summer berries. *Elderflower Vinegar*,
page 18, complements seasonal asparagus.

Elderberries: Use as soon as possible in
jams, jellies, vinegars, chutneys, sauces, pies,
pickled in brine, and *Pontack Sauce*, page 97.
Stripping berries from stems is tricky, so
freeze them and the frozen berries will fall
off with ease. Elderberries retain their shape
even after cooking at high temperature.

Folklore:
Where to begin? The
elder is steeped in
folklore, from its
witches' form to
gypsies avoiding the
wood for fires, and
in its native name,
Judas. Judas Iscariot
is said to have
hanged himself
from an elder tree.

Country folklore
suggests that the
leaves keep flies
away, and that
cattle shelter under
elder trees for
this reason.

Elderflower water is
used as a cosmetic,
and myth has it
that girls who wash
with the blossom will
gain in beauty.
Alas, this one may
be too late for me, but
heigh-ho, the fall
berries are a rich
source of vitamin C.

Wild Notes

Let your pancakes follow the seasons: try other flower blossoms (a small handful of petals that are free from uninvited, tiny visitors) such as damson, sloe, cherry, and hawthorn in the spring. Sweet cicely is also in flower in late spring, and in the later summer, you can use wild rose petals.

Elderflower SCOTCH PANCAKES

This recipe uses individual delicate flowers, bringing the essence of midsummer to your stove. Later in the season, add flower seeds. Hogweed seeds add a crunch, and a small handful of sweet cicely seeds a hint of aniseed. Serve with wild berries.

Makes 20 (depending on size)

What to do:

1 Shake the elderflowers well to remove any insects, then carefully remove the tiny, lace-like flowers, and put them into a bowl.

2 Sift the flour and baking powder into a mixing bowl and add the sugar. Make a well in the center, and pop the egg in. Using a small whisk, beat the ingredients together and slowly mix in the milk. Beat the batter so that it is smooth and without lumps. You may not need all of the millk—the mix needs to be thick, not runny, batter.

3 Beat the batter well until it is smooth and free of lumps, then gently fold in the elderflowers.

4 Heat a skillet (frying pan) with a knob of butter (do not allow it to brown) and drop a scant tablespoonful of the batter into the pan (it can be easier to put the batter into a measuring cup and slowly pour the batter into the skillet from the cup). When the pancake puffs up and starts to bubble, flip it over with a spatula (palette knife). Cook for another minute until the pancake puffs up and the underside is golden. Repeat until you have used all the batter, adding additional butter as necessary. Wrap the pancakes in a clean dish towel to keep warm.

What to forage and find:
* 3 elderflower heads, unwashed
* ¾ cup (100g) self-rising flour
* 1 teaspoon baking powder
* 2 tablespoons (25g) superfine (caster) sugar
* 1 medium egg
* Generous ½ cup (125ml) milk
* Butter, for greasing
* Honey or syrup and bilberries,

Flowers & Blossom

17

Blossom adds summer scent to vinegars and some add and even change color, too. *Rosa rugosa* petals produce rosy pink vinegar, which makes a refreshing pink drink when mixed with soda or sparkling water. Older cookery recipes add two tablespoons of vinegar in place of citric acid to cordials.

Elderflower VINEGAR

Makes 4 small bottles

What to forage and find:
* 20 elderflower heads, dry and warmed by the sun* (see below)
* Zest of ½ small lime
* Approximately 2½ cups (600ml) cider vinegar

*10 heads initially and an additional 10, ten days later (i.e. 20 over 2 pickings).

What to do:
1 Shake 10 elderflower heads well, pick the tiny flowers from the heads, and pack them into a large, sterilized, wide-necked jam jar.

2 Cut 2 small lengths of lime zest, avoiding the pith, and add this to the jar. Pour the cider vinegar over the flowers, and fill to the brim, sealing with a vinegar-proof lid.

3 Leave the elderflowers steeping in the vinegar in a warm place for 10 days, shaking occasionally.

4 Strain the vinegar through a nylon sieve, and replace the steeped elderflowers with 10 fresh ones. Pour the vinegar back over the elderflowers, and top up with more vinegar if necessary. Repeat step 3.

5 Strain the vinegar through a jelly bag (or a paper coffee filter) into a clean pitcher (jug) and pour into sterilized bottles. Seal with vinegar-proof lids, label, and store in a cool, dry place.

Wild Notes

When I can find it, I prefer to use rice vinegar for floral and herb vinegars, but cider vinegar is more readily available in rural Scotland. Use elderflower vinegar in vinaigrettes, pickles, and drinks. It's delicious on strawberries, or add a splash to gooseberry and rhubarb crumbles, or a Pavlova, before adding the cornstarch (cornflour).

Two teaspoons of elderflower vinegar mixed with a teaspoon of runny honey and some boiling water is a cold comforter, and diluted with sparkling water, it makes a very refreshing summer drink.

You could try using meadowsweet later in the season, or violets in spring (page 35). I sometimes use champagne vinegar with violets simply because it is one of my favorite flowers.

Other flowers that you might like to add to vinegar include primrose, lilac, honeysuckle, linden (lime) blossom, and wild cherry blossom.

Wild fruit and blossom curds are easy to make. Follow the seasons and add scent with blossom and crunch with wild seeds. You could also replace the gooseberries and elderflowers with ½ cup (100ml) juiced sea-buckthorn berries to make a tart orange curd in the fall.

Wild Elderflower and GOOSEBERRY CURD

Makes 1½–2 jars, depending on size

What to forage and find:
* 1 lb (450g) wild gooseberries, washed
* 2 elderflower heads (well shaken, not washed)
* 3 tablespoons *Elderflower Cordial*, page 20
* ¾ stick (85g) unsalted butter
* Generous cup (225g) superfine (caster) sugar
* 3 eggs + 2 yolks, lightly beaten

What to do:
1 Simmer the gooseberries in a saucepan with the elderflower heads and cordial until soft.

2 Remove the elderflowers, and briefly purée the gooseberries until smooth. Push the gooseberries through a sieve (to remove skins and seeds) into a heat-resistant mixing bowl.

3 Put the bowl over a pan of simmering water. Add the butter and sugar, and stir until the sugar has dissolved and the butter has melted.

4 Remove the bowl from the heat, cool slightly, and whisk in the lightly beaten eggs. Return the bowl to the pan, and then stir over gentle heat until the mixture thickens and coats the back of a wooden spoon.

5 Pour into warm, dry, sterilized jars, cool, seal, and label. Refrigerate and use within 2 weeks.

Flowers & Blossom

Elderflower CORDIAL

This floral cordial captures the summer scent of the midday hedgerow in a bottle—the essence of summer. Use undiluted as you cook, add splashes to cocktails, or dilute with soda or sparkling water. Children will love homemade frozen elderflower ice lollies.

What to do:

1 Shake the elderflowers well to remove any insects, and put them into a clean bucket or large bowl.

2 Thinly slice the lemons, and add them to the elderflowers.

3 Measure the sugar and water into a saucepan over low heat to dissolve the sugar.

4 Dissolve the citric acid in the sugar syrup, then carefully pour the syrup over the elderflowers and lemons. Cover with a clean cloth and leave for 2–3 days.

5 Carefully strain the cordial through a sieve lined with cheesecloth (muslin) into a large pitcher (jug), and pour into sterilized bottles. Store the bottles in a refrigerator, or, as I do, pour into small plastic bottles, freeze, and defrost as required.

Makes a generous 2 quarts (2 liters)

What to forage and find:

* 25 elderflower heads, insect-free
* 4 unwaxed lemons, scrubbed
* 5 cups (1kg) superfine (caster) sugar
* 5 cups (1.2 liters) boiling water
* 2 oz (55g) citric acid

About Wild Honeysuckle

Lonicera periclymenum

FAIR flower, that dost so comely grow,
Hid in this silent, dull retreat,
Untouched thy honied blossoms blow,
Unseen thy little branches greet:
No roving foot shall crush thee here,
No busy hand provoke a tear.
The Wild Honeysuckle by Philip Freneau,
reprinted from *An American Anthology*

Colloquial name:
Woodbine

Where to find:
There are many cultivated varieties of
honeysuckle, but a wild one is a sight to
behold as it rambles over hedgerows,
scrubland, and cliffs. In the Outer Hebrides,
I've even spied it clambering over shaded
rocks. The wild blossom attracts bees and
butterflies, and is particularly strong on a still
night; moths are said to be attracted to the
heady perfume from over a quarter of a mile
away. Small wonder that generations of
children have "sucked honey" from the
beautiful flowers.

How to forage and gather:
This summer blossom is delicate, so harvest
it carefully to make refreshing floral tea,
syrups, cordials, and vinegar. Use scissors
and a light touch to snip the blossoms
from the bush; their fragility will be all too
apparent. A plastic bag containing a damp
cloth will keep the blossoms from drying
out, but I suspect that many will have
disintegrated by the time you reach home.
Like many other edible flowers, you can
freeze them if you are busy, and then use
them at a later date.

How to use:
Cook with wild honeysuckle blossom for
culinary delights (see *Salmon Poached in
Wild Honeysuckle*, page 26) but don't cook
with the berries, which are toxic. The science
magic that happens (as it does with rose
petals) when lime or lemon juice is added
to wild honeysuckle blossom water is as
intoxicating as the blossom scent—the
sheer pinkness of this experiment is exciting.

The frequent visits of bees to wild
honeysuckle suggest that it is an intricate
part of our food chain, but how do I describe
its taste? My *Wild Honeysuckle Jelly*, page 24,
was certainly sweet and thickly gelatinous
(honeysuckle must contain lots of pectin) but
in the words of one of my children, "it tastes
of the countryside."

Mrs M. Grieve in *A Modern Herbal* extols
the expectorant and laxative properties of
honeysuckle.

Wild Honeysuckle and SORREL SORBET

Sheer deliciousness and science magic—the honeysuckle blossom water turns pink when the lime is added to it, while the sorrel introduces a sharp twist to the sweetness.

What to do:

1 Put the honeysuckle blossoms in a bowl with the boiling water, cover, and leave to steep overnight.

2 Strain the liquid into a saucepan and add the sugar. Heat over low heat to slowly dissolve the sugar, then boil rapidly for 3–4 minutes to thicken. You should be left with about 2 scant cups (450ml) of liquid.

3 Add the lime juice and here is the magic: it turns PINK.

4 Add the finely chopped sorrel and churn in an ice-cream machine until it is frozen.

5 If you are making this without an ice-cream machine, put the honeysuckle mixture into a freezer-safe container and freeze until slushy. Return the mixture to the bowl, beat well (or whiz in a food processor), and return to the freezer. Repeat this process until you can't see any ice crystals, and then freeze until frozen. Eat this smooth pink sorbet as soon as possible—it will melt quickly.

Makes a generous 2 quarts (2 liters)

What to forage and find:
* 4 handfuls (50g) wild honeysuckle blossoms (green bits removed)
* 2½ cups (600ml) boiling water
* 2½ cups (250g) superfine (caster) sugar, to taste
* Juice of 1 small lime
* 2 small sorrel leaves, rolled and finely sliced

Wild Honeysuckle JELLY

Perhaps this floral jelly tastes of honey because I'm reminded that Roo gave the honey-loving Winnie the Pooh a bouquet of honeysuckle when he was stuck in Rabbit's front doorway (*Winnie the Pooh* by A. A. Milne).

Makes 4 small jellies

What to forage and find:
* 2 leaves gelatin (to set 1¼ cups/300ml)
* Scant ½ cup (100ml) *Wild Honeysuckle Syrup*, page 26
* Scant 1 cup (200ml) water
* Juice of ½ lemon

What to do:
1 Soak the gelatin in cold water for 3–4 minutes until soft.

2 In a saucepan, heat the honeysuckle syrup, water, and lemon juice, and bring to a boil. Leave to cool for a minute.

3 Squeeze any excess water from the gelatin, and add to the pan. Stir well to dissolve the gelatin, then pour the honeysuckle jelly into small ramekins or glasses. Refrigerate until the jellies have set.

Wild Notes

Substitute other wildflower blossoms for the honeysuckle to make different wildflower jellies.

Wild Honeysuckle TEA

Many leaves and blossoms can be used to make wines and beers, but the simplest way of enjoying them is infused in teas or "tisanes." Some blossoms and leaves are stronger than others, and, as with making flower and herb sugars, your nose will probably help you decide the blossom to water ratio.

Makes 4 small bottles

What to forage and find:
* Handful of insect-free wild honeysuckle blossoms
* Boiling water

What to do:
1 Place the blossom in a mug and fill with boiling water. Cover with a saucer and leave to infuse for at least an hour.

2 Strain and reheat before drinking.

This idea can be adapted for use with any edible scented flower or leaf. Sometimes I add a slice of lemon, lime, or ginger. Iced Elderflower and Lemon Tea is particularly delicious. Out of season, frozen or dried blossoms and leaves can be used.

Wild Notes

Crush 2 heaping teaspoons of rose hips or hawthorn berries, put them in a pan with a mug of boiling water, and simmer over low heat for 20 minutes. Strain the berries through a sieve, and pour the remaining liquid into a mug. Sweeten with a flower syrup (e.g. honeysuckle) or honey to taste.

SALMON poached in *Wild Honeysuckle*

Poaching salmon in foraged honeysuckle blossom is a deliciously fragrant and healthy way to cook the fish, and it applies just as well to ham and poultry.

Serves 4

What to forage and find:
* Lady's handful of wild honeysuckle (4–5 blossoms)
* 4 salmon fillets, about 1 lb (450g)
* Water to cover the salmon
* 4 tablespoons *Honeysuckle Syrup* (see below)
* Juice of ½ small lime
* 4 borage flowers, washed and dried
* Salad leaves and lime wedges, to serve

What to do:

1 Fill a wide, shallow saucepan with water (just enough to cover the salmon fillets.) Add the honeysuckle blossoms, and bring the water to a boil. When the water is "just" at the point of simmer, add the salmon fillets, cover with a lid, and remove the pan from the heat. The salmon will poach in the cooling water. It is important not to overcook salmon.

2 Meanwhile, heat the honeysuckle syrup with the lime juice, and wait for the culinary magic—the syrup will go pink. Reduce the syrup by over half until it is thick and syrupy.

3 Remove the cooked salmon fillets from the poaching liquid with a fish spatula, and place them on a serving platter. Allow to cool and then thickly glaze the fillets with the honeysuckle syrup using a pastry brush. Decorate each salmon fillet with a few fresh borage flowers (or other edible flower) if desired. Serve with salad leaves and a lime wedge.

Wild Honeysuckle syrup

This is one of my favorite syrups to drizzle over ice cream. If you keep one or two small plastic bottles of it in the freezer, you can glaze your Christmas ham in wild summer blossom.

Makes 1 small bottle

What to forage and find:
* 2 large handfuls of wild honeysuckle (12–15 blossoms)
* Scant 1½ cups (350ml) boiling water (50ml will evaporate or soak into the blossom)
* 1 cup (200g) superfine (caster) sugar

What to do:

1 Allow the honeysuckle blossom to steep in the water for as long as possible (at least 8 hours).

2 Strain the blossom liquid well, and squeeze the blossom to ensure that you have as much liquid as possible.

3 Put the blossom water into a saucepan, and add the sugar.

4 Dissolve the sugar over low heat, then boil rapidly to reduce and thicken the syrup to about ¾ cup (175ml).

Wild Notes

I have used a lower ratio of sugar to flower blossom water in this recipe because honeysuckle is sweet. The resulting syrup is consequently thinner than some of the other blossom syrups. Honeysuckle syrup can be reduced further to thicken, if desired. Dilute the syrup with water, or Prosecco in drinks, serve on oatmeal (porridge), drizzle on ice cream, or use it when cooking tart fruits (e.g. quince).

Honeysuckle syrup can also be rubbed on to gammon steaks, or indeed into cooked hams before the final oven roasting (in place of, for example, maple syrup)— the result is sweetly moist.

About Sweet Violet

Viola odorata

Where to find:

The majestic color of the tiny violet brightens the hedgerows in spring, beside the greens and whites of the countryside. You will also find them in woods, on grassy banks, and on heathland (even on grassy rocks). Ironically, they aren't always violet, but may be blue, white, or red, although red is a rarity.

Violets may not be easy to see; perhaps this is why the Victorians associated the flower with modesty (the shrinking violet). I've often found them under the leaves of less bashful celandines.

Once located, there is usually a mate or two on the patch. *The Gentle Art of Cookery* gives a recipe for *Violet Nosegays*, which is doubtlessly a relic from the Victorian tussie mussie (posy) heyday. In Roman times, the flower was associated with mourning and put onto graves as a demonstration of continued affection.

How to forage and gather:

The sweet violet is not to be mistaken for the common dog violet, so named because it is not only common but without fragrance—only fit for dogs. Dog and heath violets are not as fragrant as the sweet violet, which is found in more open habitats, including churchyards—I admit to having foraged in full view of the minister and congregation. Take a small glass jar with a lid for violet collection. Primroses often grow nearby, and they crystallize well, too.

How to use:

Cooking with violets is one of the most destructive things that I do, spoiling the beauty of the countryside for selfish deliciousness, but my bottles are small, as are my glasses of pink gin. The tiny, heart-shaped leaves can be used in salads or cakes, and were used to thicken sauces and broths. Mark Twain said of the sweet violet, "Forgiveness is the fragrance that the violet sheds on the heel that has crushed it."

For the candy-loving girl there are *Charbonnel et Walker* violet creams, or an inexpensive "Parma Violet." Violets can also be used instead of rose to flavor Turkish delight (I confess, I add a touch of food coloring). Crystallized violets and syrup will extend the season of spring in your pantry or store cupboard, but, if I am honest, mine rarely last for long.

I don't use preservatives, and my drying methods are amateur; although I do know how to remove the crystals that collect in wild flower and herb syrup bottles (see *Sweet Violet Syrup* recipe, page 38.) The forager cooks with the season, and the more prudent prepare for a winter famine, but my philosophy is: Go with the seasonal flow—violets in spring, not winter.

Folklore:

In the UK, Mothering Sunday, the fourth Sunday in Lent, was a holiday for girls in domestic service. On that day, they would visit their mothers, taking gifts of a posy of violets and a Simnel cake.

Violet DRINKING CHOCOLATE

The fairy spirit Puck used violet juices in *A Midsummer Night's Dream* to encourage love, so who knows what will happen if you add violets to hot chocolate, dark or white.

Makes 2 mugs

What to forage and find:
* 2 oz (55g) good-quality bittersweet (dark) chocolate (minimum 70% cocoa solids)
* 1¾ cups (400ml) whole milk
* 2 teaspoons *Sweet Violet Syrup*, page 38
* 2 crystallized violets

What to do:

1 Break the chocolate into squares and put it into a food processor. Blend briefly to grate the chocolate (with the funnel lid in place, and the machine held firmly to stop it moving).

2 Heat the milk and violet syrup over low heat, and when warm, whisk in the grated chocolate. Whisk well to ensure that the chocolate has melted. Pour into mugs, pop a crystallized violet on top, and serve immediately.

Sweet Violet GIN

This recipe was discovered by accident while making violet syrup. The ever-resourceful Dr Bird, my husband, suggested gin as a better solvent. I was dubious, and indeed the gin went orange, not violet, but when I added tonic (on a "waste not, want not" basis), my gin turned pink.

Serving number depends on how much you like to dilute your gin

What to forage and find:
* 6 handfuls of sweet violets over two pickings
* 1 cup (250ml) gin
* Tonic water (optional)

What to do:

1 Dust the violets with a dry pastry brush.

2 Pour the gin into a measuring cup and add three handfuls of violets. Cover with a plate.

3 The following day, add the second picking of violets to the gin, and cover. The violets with color will float, and as the violets lose color, they sink—fascinating, and I haven't an explanation for this.

4 After 3–4 days, the violets will be white and the gin will be orange/light brown. You can strain the violets if you want to, but I leave the violets floating in a clear bottle, and strain the gin as I use it.

Flowers & Blossom

My paternal grandmother lived by London's famous Kew Gardens, and a childhood treat would be a visit to *The Original Maids Of Honour Tearoom*. Kew, synonymous with flowers and the *Maids of Honour* cake, was my inspiration for this recipe. Making 12 small tarts is in keeping with the style of the authentic *Maids of Honour*, but you could make just one larger tart, using a pan with a diameter of 8 inches (20cm) if you wish.

CUSTARD TARTS with *Violets*

Wild Notes

Violet syrup in the pastry is not necessary; just use water if you haven't any syrup. You might like to add a few shredded, washed, and dried violet leaves (chiffonade), either to the pastry or custard or both. Alternatively, use small heart-shaped leaves on top of the tart for decoration.

Makes 12 individual tarts or one 8-inch (20cm) tart

What to forage and find:
For the crust:
* 1½ cups (200g) all-purpose (plain) flour
* ½ stick (50g) butter
* 3 tablespoons + 1 teaspoon (50g) lard
* 1 egg yolk
* 1 teaspoon *Sweet Violet Syrup*, page 38, mixed with 3 tablespoons water (see *Wild Notes*, right)

For the filling:
* 5 eggs
* ¼ cup (50g) superfine (caster) sugar
* 1 scant cup (200ml) heavy (double) cream
* 3 tablespoons fresh violets

What to do:
1 Preheat the oven to 400°F (200°C/gas mark 6).

2 To make the pastry, sift the flour into a bowl and rub in the fats until the mixture resembles breadcrumbs.

3 Add the egg yolk to the violet water and then add enough liquid to the pastry so that it binds. You may not need all of the liquid.

4 Knead the pastry briefly until smooth. Wrap in plastic wrap (clingfilm) and refrigerate for 20 minutes.

5 Roll the pastry out thinly to line the 12 tart pans. Bake blind (line the pans with foil and baking beans) in the oven for 7–8 minutes. Remove the foil and beans, and bake for another 3 minutes until the base is golden. (If making one large tart, bake blind for 10 minutes with the beans, then for 5–6 minutes to crisp the base.) Take the pans out of the oven and reduce the temperature to 300°F (150°C/gas mark 2).

6 To make the filling, lightly beat the eggs, add the sugar and cream, and beat briefly.

7 Scatter two handfuls of the violets over the prepared tart pans and pour in most of the cream mixture. Put the tart pans on a baking sheet and put the baking sheet in the oven. Add the remaining cream mixture evenly, and scatter the remaining violets over the top of the tarts. (This avoids overflow spillage *en route* to the oven.) Bake for about 10–12 minutes (40 minutes for one large tart), until the custard is just firm; it will continue setting after baking.

Wild Notes

For Wild Rose Macarons, use crystallized rose petals in place of violets, and add crystallized wild rose petals to the cream.

The primrose cream could also be replaced with crystallized violet cream.

In summer, sandwich the macarons together with wild raspberries, wild cherries, strawberries, or Wild Elderflower and Gooseberry Curd (page 19).

Macarons lend themselves to any forager's kitchen and will also tempt visitors on gluten-free diets. Use any wild blossom sugars or crystallized flowers to make the macarons, and fold puréed wild berries into the filling, or add tiny wild strawberries whole. Infuse blossoms such as linden (lime) with a little creamy milk and add it to the butter cream. Wild macarons simply rock with invention.

Violet MACARONS with *Primrose Cream*

Makes 8 macaron sandwiches

What to forage and find:
* 1 tablespoon crystallized violets (see *Crystallized Flowers*, page 15)
* Generous 1¾ cup (175g) sifted confectioners' (icing) sugar
* ¾ cup (100g) blanched almonds
* 3 extra large (large UK) egg whites
* ⅓ cup (75g) superfine (caster) sugar
* Violet food coloring (optional)
* 24 violet leaves, washed and patted dry

For the primrose cream filling:
* ⅔ cup (150ml) lightly whipped heavy (double) cream
* 1 tablespoon crushed crystallized primroses (see *Crystallized Flowers*, page 15)

What to do:
1 Preheat the oven to 325°F (160°C/gas mark 3).

2 Line two baking sheets with parchment paper.

3 Finely blend the violets, confectioners' (icing) sugar, and almonds in a food processor.

4 Whisk the egg whites in a clean bowl until they are firm, and gradually whisk in the superfine (caster) sugar and violet food coloring, if using. Whisk until the meringue is shiny.

5 Carefully fold in half of the ground almond, sugar and violet mixture, then fold in the remainder.

6 Place a small blob of filling mixture under each corner of parchment paper-lined baking sheets to hold the paper in place, then either pipe or spoon 16 flat circles about 1¼–1½ inches (3–4cm) across (the macarons will spread during cooking). Place a violet leaf on top of each macaron. Tap the baking sheet three times, turn the tray, and repeat to flatten the macarons. Leave to stand at room temperature for 15 minutes before baking (to allow a skin to form).

7 Bake for 15 minutes until the macarons are just set. Leave to cool on the baking paper, and remove when cold.

8 Fold the crushed crystallized primroses into the whipped cream, and use 1–2 teaspoonsful of the mixture to sandwich two macarons together.

QUAIL EGGS pickled in *Violet* vinegar

This recipe preserves tiny quail eggs with a hint of the fragrance of spring.

Makes 1 small jar

What to forage and find:
* 10 quail eggs
* Approximately 1 cup (250ml) *Violet Vinegar*, see below
* ½ teaspoon pink peppercorns
* ½ teaspoon coriander seeds
* 1 allspice berry

What to do:
1 Cook the eggs in simmering water for 2½ minutes to hard boil. Put them in a colander and rinse under cold water. Peel the shells as soon as they are cool enough to handle. I find it easier to remove the shells under running cold water.

2 Mix the rest of the ingredients in a measuring cup (jug).

3 Put the cold quail eggs into a small 9 fl oz (250ml) jar, then pour the violet vinegar and spices over the eggs

4 Seal the jar with a vinegar-proof lid, and store for a month before eating.

Wild Notes

Newly made violet vinegar is a lovely shade of pink for a few days, but will turn orange. This has an interesting effect on the quail eggs, which take on the color of hens' eggshells— simply stunning.

Violet VINEGAR

Perfectly pink vinegar. This is such a simple idea it doesn't really justify a recipe.

Makes 1 generous cup (250ml)

What to forage and find:
* 1 handful sweet violets
* 1 generous cup (250ml) rice vinegar

What to do:
1 Remove any green stems from the violets and leave them to dry on a sunny windowsill. Then put them in a small, sterilized jam jar.

2 Fill the jar with rice vinegar, and seal with a sterile, vinegar-proof lid.

3 Put the jar on a sunny windowsill for 3–4 days, until the violets have lost their color. Strain to remove the violets, then return the violet vinegar to the jar or a sterilized bottle.

Use in fruit chutneys, vinaigrettes, and light marinades, or see *Quail Eggs Pickled in Violet Vinegar*, above.

Wild Notes

Replace the violets with segmented clover flowers, lilac, dog rose petals, honeysuckle, or linden (lime) blossoms. To make garlic vinegar, use ramps (wild garlic) flowers. You can make wild herb vinegars using wild thyme, marjoram, and mint leaves and flowers. Chive flowers add both rosy color and flavor to vinegar. Flowers and leaves should be dry, and vinegar acidity at least 5% for successful preservation.

Flowers & Blossom

Sweet Violet FAIRY BUTTER

This recipe is an adaptation of Mrs Beeton's *Fairy Butter*. It reminds me of a sweet clotted cream and is a wonderful addition to afternoon tea.

Makes 1 small bowl

What to forage and find:
* 2 hard-boiled egg yolks
* Heaping tablespoon sifted confectioners' (icing) sugar
* 1 tablespoon violet water (see recipe for *Flower Blossom Water*, *Wild Notes*, page 39)
* ½ stick (50g) soft unsalted butter

What to do:
1 Put the egg yolks, confectioners' (icing) sugar, and violet water in a bowl and mix with a fork.

2 Add the butter, mash the ingredients together with a fork or potato masher, and refrigerate until just firm.

3 Push the sweet fairy butter through a sieve (this gives the delicate fairy effect) and serve with warm scones, Scotch pancakes (a sweeter, smaller version of American pancakes), or crumpets.

Wild Notes

Replace the violet flavor with other floral waters or use a teaspoon of blossom cordial.

Violet BUTTERCREAM

This buttercream recipe uses violet syrup but, as with so many of the other recipes in this book, it lends itself to adaptation by the creative cook. Many edible leaves and blossoms can be used to scent and flavor syrup which can then be added to buttercream.

Makes 1 lb (450g)

What to forage and find:
* Scant 1½ sticks (150g) soft unsalted butter
* 3 cups (300g) sifted confectioners' (icing) sugar
* About 1 tablespoon *Sweet Violet Syrup*, page 38

What to do:
1 Put the softened butter in a bowl and beat in half of the confectioners' (icing) sugar.

2 Beat in the remaining sugar and enough violet syrup to make a smooth, spreadable paste.

Wild Notes

Decorate with angelica or sweet cicely and crystallized violet or rose petals (see Crystallized Flowers, page 15). You can use any syrup in buttercream frosting (icing).

Sweet Violet SYRUP

A lovely recipe for capturing the scent of woodland and meadow blossom. Sometimes syrups crystallize and the color fades, so store them where you can keep a watchful eye on any sugar-crystal gremlins.

Makes 1 small bottle

What to forage and find:
* 3 handfuls of violets
* ½ cup (125ml) boiling water
* 1 cup (200g) superfine (caster) sugar
* Red and blue food coloring

What to do:

1 Remove any green bits from the violets (tweezers are useful). Crush the violets and put them in a sterilized jar.

2 Pour the boiling water over the violets, cover, and leave for 24 hours. Strain the violet water into a pitcher (jug).

3 Put the sugar into a heavy-based saucepan and add the strained violet water. DO NOT STIR. Cook slowly over low heat until the sugar has dissolved; this may take 10–15 minutes. Bring the syrup to a boil briefly.

4 Remove the pan from the heat and pour the syrup into a pitcher, cool briefly, and add a little red and blue food coloring until it is the desired color. Pour into a sterilized jam jar, or small bottle, and store in a dry place.

5 This is delicious on ice cream, in icing and buttercream frosting (see *Sweet Violet Fairy Butter*, page 36), in sparkling wine or water, junkets, milk shakes, and our Scottish favorite, on oatmeal (porridge).

Wild Notes

Do experiment with alternative wild edible blossom and flower syrups using a liquid to sugar ratio of ½ cup (125ml) liquid to 1 cup (200g) sugar. Here are some suggestions that I've had success with: clover, meadowsweet, elderflower, dandelion, wild cherry, dog rose petals, lilac, and hawthorn, and here is one that I wouldn't recommend—rowan blossom.

Sugar syrups can prove irksome to make. Some swear that a copper pan stops the sugar recrystallizing; others will make syrups in a bain marie. I use a shallow, heavy-based pan that allows the sugar to dissolve slowly. Do not be tempted to stir the sugar as it dissolves because a stray grain of sugar on the side of the pan will crystallize. Pastry chefs wash the pan sides down with a damp pastry brush. It is probably prudent to put the sugar into the pan before adding the water.

Ensure the sugar has dissolved completely before boiling the syrup. I don't use a sugar thermometer, but the higher the temperature the syrup reaches, the thicker the set.

I store syrup in jam jars or small glass bottles, and if the syrup does crystallize, I put the bottle on its side and reheat it in a pan of gently simmering water until the syrup is clear. Don't be tempted to do this until you need to, especially if you've added food coloring because the color may change. I have to say my biggest disappointment was the addition of food coloring to this recipe. I tested it countless times, in the hope that the violet syrup would remain bluish-purple, but eventually resorted to food coloring. However, I discovered Violet Gin, page 29, in the process.

About Flower Blossom Waters

My paternal grandmother encouraged my love of wildflowers. I still have my copy of *A First Book of Wild Flowers*, which she gave me for my seventh birthday. The book conjures up scented, summer hedgerow memories of sweet-smelling honeysuckle tangled with jagged dog rose. My sister Nicki and I have less fragrant memories of jars of browning rose petals soaking in cold water for weeks. We didn't quite get the hang of it—the secret is: boiling water, flowers, evaporation, and distilled flower water. Flower waters, one of the oldest toiletries, were used in the Middle Ages for cooking. Today, they are used more ubiquitously in Middle Eastern recipes—bring on a revival, I say. Used sparingly, blossom waters add flavor to rice pudding, thickened cream, yogurts, fresh and dried fruits, sorbets, frostings and icings, cocktails, and sparkling mineral water. The waters make a floral-intense base for flower syrups, which can be used in ice creams or milkshakes.

In Scotland, the bright, yellow gorse flower cheers up a rainy spring day, and the plant is in flower throughout the year. In *The Return of the Native*, Thomas Hardy describes gorse in season when Clym becomes a furze (gorse) cutter. I use gorse blossom water to add delicate flavor to icing on cakes or cookies, but a few fragrant drops from a cold bottle on the face will refresh a cook on a hot day.

Gorse WATER

Make wildflower waters using any scented, edible flower: lilac, rose, violet, sweet cicely, hawthorn, elderflower, or meadowsweet. Ensure that you go for scent, not color, because the distilled water is clear.

Makes about ⅓ cup (75ml)

What to forage and find:
* About 6 large handfuls (50g / ¼ plastic grocery [carrier] bag) gorse blossoms, collected in sunshine
* Boiling water to cover the blossoms

What to do:

1 Rinse the flowers with cold water and strain through a colander.

2 Put a trivet (I use a small, heat-resistant ramekin, but a metal jam jar lid will suffice) into a saucepan and heap the blossoms around the ramekin. Pour in enough boiling water to cover the gorse flowers. Balance a small, sterile jam jar on the trivet and invert the pan lid to cover. The pan lid needs to sit heavily on the pan without any vent for steam to escape.

3 Heat the pan, and when the water boils, put a bowl full of ice cubes on top of the lid (or weigh the lid down with freezer blocks). As the steam hits the cold lid, it condenses, and will fall into the jam jar. Replenish the ice or ice block as necessary, and heat until the water surrounding the flowers has evaporated and condensed—this will take about 15 minutes.

4 Remove the jar of gorse water, seal with a lid, and refrigerate. Use within a couple of months.

> ## Wild Notes
> For yellow gorse frosting (icing), simply boil the gorse blossom in water, strain, and use the colored water with sugar in icing.

About Wild Cherry

Prunus avium

I toyed with the idea of including wild cherries with other members of the *Prunus* family, namely: the damsons, bullaces, and sloes, but the wild cherry is my favorite tree, and so majestic, that I decided it must stand alone.

Colloquial names:

Gean, Mazzard, Murrys

Loveliest of trees, the cherry now
Is hung with bloom along the bough,
And stands about the woodland ride
Wearing white for Eastertide.

Now, of my three score years and ten,
Twenty will not come again,
And take from seventy springs a score,
It only leaves me fifty more.

And since to look at things in bloom
Fifty springs are little room,
About the woodlands I will go
To see the cherry hung with snow.
A. E. Housman, *A Shropshire Lad* 1896

Where to find:

This splendid tree banks hedgerows and is found in woodland. Older trees have huge, umbrella-like branches that can almost touch the ground. "Wearing white for Eastertide" describes the spring cherry blossom well, and it's a haven for bumblebees, but give it a cruel wind, and the tiny cherry petals flutter like bride's confetti to the ground. This splash of spring color is, for me, reminiscent of our fragility—the fleeting nature of life.

How to forage and gather:

The midsummer fruits color from yellow, to orange, to almost black when ripe, but pick them quickly because the birds like them, too. In my experience, some cherries are

sweeter than others, I am unsure why. Be prepared to spend some time filling your basket, because the cherries are tiny. Leave the stems on cherries and they will keep fresh for longer; they freeze well.

How to use:

I love cooking with tiny cherries, or "geans" as we call them in Scotland. I make cherry brandy and use the berries in hedgerow jellies. The berries are small and fiendish to pit, so the easiest-to-make recipes use berries that are cooked and pitted when soft, or puréed through a nylon sieve—a wee bit of effort, but well worth it. Make wild glacé cherries to add to Christmas cake and mincemeat.

As for the blossoms, I eat them and I am alive, but I have come across cherry bark and leaf warnings, so best not to take a chance with these.

Folklore:

In Scotland, in May 2011, freak storms snapped the crown of my favorite wild cherry, but the remaining boughs broke into flower, which is wonderful news. In the spring following the British storms of 1987, wind-damaged cherry trees were found on the ground in horizontal blossom. The tree must be hardy!

In Japan, where cherry blossom is the national flower, the cherry represents beauty, courtesy, and modesty.

In the US, legend tells that the young George Washington was said to have cut down his father's favorite tree, but owned up to the misdemeanor. "My son, that you should not be afraid to tell the truth is more to me than a thousand trees! Yes—though they were blossomed with silver and had leaves of the purest gold!"

Wild Cherry Blossom PANNA COTTA

Decorate this panna cotta with crystalized edible wild flowers, chopped wild nuts, or seeds squirreled away in the fall; or, in season, serve with wild strawberries.

What to do:

1 Pack the cherry blossoms (the stamens too) into a jam jar and add the milk. Refrigerate for 48 hours.

2 Soak the gelatin leaves in cold water for 3–4 minutes to soften.

3 Strain the cherry-blossom-infused milk. Put the strained milk, cream, and sugar into a heavy-based saucepan. Heat over low heat to dissolve the sugar. Do not boil.

4 Squeeze any excess water from the softened gelatin, and add the gelatin to the cream. Stir well over the lowest heat to dissolve the gelatin completely.

5 Lightly oil the molds. Put a violet in the base of each of 4 dariole molds or ramekins, pour a little of the panna cotta

on top, and refrigerate until it has begun to set. Divide the remaining panna cotta (which has remained at room temperature) between the molds, and refrigerate until set.

6 Briefly dip the molds in warm water, and turn out onto individual plates. Serve drizzled with *Sweet Violet* or *Cherry Blossom Syrup*, page 38, or poached rhubarb and sweet cicely.

Wild Notes

Replace the wild cherry blossoms with hawthorn blossoms, honeysuckle, gorse, clover, violets, linden (lime) blossoms, or dog rose.

Makes 4

What to forage and find:

* Enough cherry blossoms to fill a jam jar
* Approximately 1½ cups (350ml) milk
* 3 sheets (leaves) gelatin (small)
* 1 generous cup (250ml) heavy (double) cream
* About 3 tablespoons (40g) superfine (caster) sugar, to taste
* 4 sweet violets, green bits removed, washed, and dried

* 4 x 3½-fl oz (100ml) dariole molds or ramekins

Flowers & Blossom

About Wild Rose and Rose Hips

Rosa rugosa

"Ring a-ring o' roses,
A pocketful of posies;
A-tishoo! A-tishoo!
We all fall down."

Colloquial names:

Dog Rose, Canker, Haggebutt, Rosa rugosa, Rosa canina, Wild Briar, Sweet Briar, Rose Hips, Heps, Rose Haws, Itchy-Coos

Where to find:

The wild rose is a delicate, miniature version of the cultivated garden rose. It grows on rambling hedgerow bushes, reaching 9 feet (3 metres) in height. The tiny petals on the solo, wild rose can vary from the lightest of pinks to dark cotton candy (candyfloss).

The flowers bloom throughout summer, but, sadly, hedgerow-cutting machines can destroy a forager's bounty in seconds and a strong wind may blow delicate petals away before the gatherer has visited.

The rose hips—scarlet oval berries with a hint of orange—can be found from late summer right through to the end of the fall.

How to forage and gather:

Flowers: Don't over-pick, and wear gardening gloves as protection from the thorny branches. Gather petals into a basket with care; a gust of wind or a jolt of the basket and the petals will be blown far and wide. A pack of antiseptic wipes in the pocket, to combat escapee thorns, is prudent.

Rose hips: Again, wear gloves as protection, and take a stick with you for tackling out-of-reach branches.

How to use:

Petals: These can be crystallized for decorations or used in syrups, vinegar, jellies, and cakes, and rosewater is said to enhance the complexion. A jar of rose sugar is a useful addition to any kitchen.

Rose hips: These can be used in hedgerow jellies and the strained juice in syrups, junkets, and mousses. Young rose leaves, like those of raspberry and blackberry, can be infused in tisanes.

Folklore:

Adaptations of The UK Ministry of Food's wartime recipe for Rosehip Syrup are still in use today. The use of a present-day food processor to blend the hips will certainly ease the chopping. UK schoolchildren continued to collect hips to make the rich in vitamin C syrup well into the 1950s. Rosehip syrup adds an intersting flavor to vinaigrettes and works well with fall fruits.

The hips contain high levels of vitamins A and B, as well as C, and over the winter months, when other vitamin-rich plants were scarce, they were an important source of nutrients for Native Americans. They also used the hips for cold remedies and muscular pains.

Rose hips strung as beads in a necklace were said to attract love, but this seems rather odd because children used the fine hairs on the rosehip seeds to make itching powder (known as itchy coos in Scotland). Dry the seeds before use (freezing rose hips and then slicing them makes the seeds easier to remove), store the fine hairs in a jar (not the seeds) and use sparingly down the back of a friend's sweater. This recipe needs testing—hopefully a schoolchild will come to my aid!

The "Five Brethren of the Rose" folklore riddle is often cited for the identification of wild roses: "two with whiskers on the side, two smooth and the last, whiskered on one side only."

This recipe is dedicated to Maxim, who spent an afternoon collecting the fragile petals to make and test this hedgerow nectar. Foraging rose petals is labor intensive. *Rosa rugosa* petals are larger than those of the dog rose and will make brighter pink cordials and syrups.

Wild Rose and ORANGE CORDIAL

What to do:

1 Put the dog rose petals in a clean bucket. Thinly slice the oranges, and add them to the petals.

2 Measure the sugar and water into a saucepan, and heat over low heat to dissolve the sugar.

3 Dissolve the citric acid in the sugar syrup, then, carefully pour the syrup over the rose petals and oranges. Cover with a clean kitchen (tea) towel, and set aside for 2–3 days.

4 Strain the cordial through a sieve lined with cheesecloth (muslin) into a large pitcher (jug), and pour into sterilized bottles. Store the bottles in a refrigerator, or as I do, pour into small plastic bottles, freeze, and defrost as required.

5 Serve with borage ice cubes and sweet cicely or lovage straws, see *Borage*, page 149.

Makes 2–3 bottles

What to forage and find:
* Half a small bucket (100g) of dog rose petals
* 2 oranges, scrubbed
* 2¼lb (1kg) superfine (caster) sugar to taste
* 1½ quarts (1.5 liters) water
* 2oz (55g) citric acid or 2 tablespoons of rose vinegar

Wild Notes

This syrup is rather sweet and it is delicious in cocktails for grown-ups, with ice cream or yogurt, in glacé icing, on fruit crumble and crepes, in summer fruit compotes, and on oatmeal (porridge).

About Meadow Flowers

I worry more about recipes that use flower blossoms than any other because of the sheer destruction of beauty for consumption. But daisies, clover, and dandelions grow everywhere.

Daisy
Bellis perennis

If I had my life to live over, I would start barefoot earlier in the spring and stay that way later in the fall. I would go to more dances. I would ride more merry-go-rounds and I would pick more daisies. Nadine Stair of Louisville, Kentucky, aged 85

Colloquial names:
Banwood, Little Star, Miss Modesty, Silver Pennies, Bairnwort

I like to think that the Scottish name for daisy—bairnwort—is associated with making daisy chains ("bairn" means child). When I was a child, I would make daisy-chain garlands and now I'm cooking with them.

Where to find:
Lawns, grass verges, and meadows. Daisies flower from spring until fall, but are at their best in midsummer. The Olde English name, "daeges-eaye" or "day's eye," reflects the way the flowers open and close with the sun.

How to forage and gather:
Daisies are a great source of pollen for insects. It is said that summer hasn't arrived until you can put your foot on seven daisies on the lawn (Mrs M. Grieve, *A Modern Herbal*). Pick young leaves, which are said to be rich in potassium, in spring. Leaves become bitter once the daisy is in flower.

How to use:
Leaves can be chopped in salads, and the flowers used for decoration. I don't rate their flavor highly, but the flowers are useful if you are looking for bulk.

Red Clover
Trifolium pratense

White Clover
Trifolium repens

Where to find:
Both red and white clovers grow in grassy places, and as is the case with other meadow flowers, attract insects. Clover flowers throughout the summer.

How to forage and gather:
Pick only young flowers in which the segments are upturned, not down, and pick before the flowers go brown. Use scissors to cut the flowers, and segment the flowers before cooking with them, thereby avoiding any green bits.

How to use:
Clover can be pickled with spiced vinegar and honey, and used in game dishes, in syrup, crystallized, or in *Carrot and Clover Cake* (page 47).

Dandelion
Taraxacum officinale

The dandelion is brave and gay
And loves to sit beside the way;
A braver thing was never seen,
To praise the grass for growing green;
You never saw a gayer thing,
To sit and smile and praise the Spring.
Frances Cornford

Colloquial names:
Clock Flower, Clocks and Watches, Wet-the-Bed, Pissy, Tiddle-Beds, Tell-Time, Priest's Crown, Swine's Snout.

Where to find:
Meadows, pastures, wasteland, grass roadsides, and in gardens.

How to forage and gather:
In early spring, as soon as you spy the leaves, pick them for salads, and like the flowers, don't gather them later than early summer. The flowers and buds will leave a sticky stain on your hands, but it washes away with ease. The dandelion attracts many insect visitors, so shake it well before gathering to make *Meadow Flower Scented Honey*, page 48. Dandelions add hugely to this recipe due to the high content of nectar and pollen, and ease of foraging, thanks to the length of its flowering season. It is the beekeeper's friend, but remember other flying visitors, too, and give the flowers a good shake before popping them into your basket.

Although the flower may be regarded as common or garden, there are lots of species. One of the main points of identification is the tooth-spiked leaves; this is where the French name for dandelion comes from—*dent de lion*. The flower is lion-like, too, with its "mane."

How to use:
Young dandelion leaves have long been regarded as a delicacy by the French, and are used in a classic salad dish with bacon and croutons. The leaves are more of a gourmet delight before the dandelion flowers. Mrs M. Grieve, in *A Modern Herbal*, talks of delicious sandwiches made from young dandelion leaves. The leaves can be bitter, not unlike chicory (endive), so you might like to blanche them, or soak them in water before eating, and then use them as you would spinach. Eat the flowers before they are fully open, i.e. buds, but don't be fooled—the flowers close at a sniff of rain, and long before the night dews. The buds are delicious in salads, vinegars, boiled, or cooked in batter. See *Wild Blossom Tempura*, page 131.

Traditionally, dandelions were used in beers and wines, but you can also make vodka, cordials, and honey. All parts of the dandelion are edible, and although I have avoided roots in this book, dandelion roots are commonly used to make coffee and tea.

Folklore:
The dandelion is a diuretic and produces ethylene, which helps to ripen fruit if a flower or two is placed in a fruit bowl. As a child, I remember blowing the fluffy seeds of the dandelion to tell the time. The number of blows to remove all of the seeds gave you the hour of the clock. I'm not sure we really believed it, but it helped to pass the time as I waited to jump the "highjump" at Holy Trinity Primary School. Folklore suggests that some people refuse to touch the flower for fear of wetting the bed (see colloquial names).

Both red and white clovers grow in grassy places and, as is the case with other meadow flowers, attract insects. Clover flowers throughout the summer, but only pick young flowers, where the flower segments are upturned (not down), and pick before the flowers go brown. Segment the flowers before cooking with them, avoiding any green bits.

CARROT and *Clover* CAKE

Serves 8

What to forage and find:
* ⅔ cup (150ml) canola (vegetable) oil
* ⅔ cup (125g) superfine (caster) sugar
* 6 clover flowers, washed and segmented
* 2 extra large (large UK) eggs
* Scant 2 cups (250g) self-rising flour
* 1 heaping teaspoon baking powder
* 1½ cups (200g) finely grated carrots

For the frosting (icing):
* 1½ cups (150g) sifted confectioners' (icing) sugar
* ½ stick (50g) soft unsalted butter
* 3 clover flowers, washed and segmented

What to do:

1 Preheat the oven to 350°F (180°C/gas mark 4).

2 Line an 8-inch (20cm) round cake pan (tin) with parchment paper.

3 Measure the oil and sugar into a bowl, add three segmented clover flowers, and beat in the eggs.

4 Sift the flour and baking powder into the bowl and add the grated carrot. Fold the flour and carrot mixture into the oil, sugar, clover, and eggs.

5 Turn the mixture into the prepared pan and bake for 40–45 minutes until the cake is firm and well risen (it will shrink away from the sides of the pan). Cool for 5 minutes, then invert the cake onto a wire rack to cool.

6 To make the frosting, sift the confectioners' sugar into a bowl and beat in the softened butter. Add most of the segmented clover flowers, reserving a few to decorate the carrot and clover cake.

7 Spread the clover frosting on top of the cold cake, and sprinkle the reserved flower segments over the top.

Wild Notes

Make the frosting using flower-infused superfine (caster) sugar—see flower and herb sugars, page 15. Also, you can use wild mountain thyme instead of clover.

Flowers & Blossom

Meadow Flower SCENTED HONEY

This honey-scented thick syrup has a golden clarity that reminds me of unspoiled, litter-free countryside with buzzing bumblebees and fluttering butterflies. Collect flowers only where they are growing prolifically. Digital scales are useful for weighing blossoms.

Makes 3 small jars

What to forage and find:
* About 8–10 small handfuls (75g) dandelion blossoms, daisies, and clover
* 1 quart (liter) boiling water
* Juice of 1 large lemon
* 1¼ lb (575g) superfine (caster) sugar

What to do:

1 Remove the dandelion flowers (don't use anything green). Segment the clover flowers, and pull the daisies from their stems (use all of the flower).

2 Put the flowers in a saucepan, cover with boiling water, boil for 1 minute, cover with a lid, then leave to steep overnight.

3 The next day, strain the flowers through a sieve, squeezing well to ensure that the maximum scented flower water is used in the syrup. Add the lemon juice to the liquid, and for each 2½ cups (600ml) of liquid, add 1 lb (450g) of sugar. I used 1¼ lb (575g).

4 Return the pan to the stovetop (hob), and dissolve the sugar over low heat, then bring the pan to a rolling boil for about 15 minutes, until the syrup is thick and resembles honey.

5 This meadow flower honey has minimal (if any) scum; if there is some, skim it off with a slotted spoon. Pour the clear syrup into warm sterilized jars. Cover and label.

Wild Notes

When I asked my daughter, Lili, to test this recipe, she couldn't find many clover flowers, in spite of spending a long time foraging. Lili's honey was made predominantly with daisies and dandelions; it was delicious, but we both agreed that the inclusion of more clover flowers adds lusciousness.

About Meadowsweet

Filipendula ulmaria

"The smell there of (Meadowsweet) makes the heart merry and joyful and delighteth the senses."
Gerard's Herball (1597)

Colloquial names:
Courtship and Matrimony, May of the Meadow, Meadow Queen

Where to find:
In spite of its name, meadowsweet favors damp land; it grows in roadside ditches in partial shade and on riverbanks. It appears in midsummer, when the elderflower is fading, and works well in elderflower recipes, thereby extending your floral scented season to early fall—Nature is so clever.

The red stems are brittle and grow 3–6 feet (1–2 metres) in height. The leaves are three-pronged; the undersides are downy, and a lighter color. The yellowish-white flowers are small, with 5–6 petals arranged in clusters, not unlike elderflowers, but they are more robust. The plant's fragrant musky scent may reach you before you spy it. The leaves have an altogether different scent from the flowers, not unlike almond.

How to forage and gather:
As for elderflower blossoms, gather on a dry and sunny day. The early leaves (before the flowers appear) can be eaten but I find them slightly bitter.

How to use:
In cordials, with summer fruits, and in recipes that ask for elderflowers. Meadowsweet has a delicious honey taste, and acts as a natural sweetener, so no need to add much sugar. The blossom dries well and makes refreshing tea. Young leaves can be infused in tisanes and in savory custards. Meadowsweet ice cream is delicious, and *Red Berries and Meadowsweet Pudding*, page 117, is a real summer treat.

Folklore:
Meadowsweet was a favorite herb of the Druids, and much used in medieval times as a strewing herb to decorate banqueting halls and churches. The strange quality of the leaves and flowers having different scents is reflected in its local name "Courtship and Matrimony." Meadowsweet gathered on Midsummer's Day was used to determine the gender of a thief: When thrown into water, if the meadowsweet sank, the thief was male; if it floated, then she was female.

Famously used in mead (hence its name), it is one of 50 ingredients in a drink called "Save," which is mentioned in Chaucer's "Knight's Tale," being called medwort or meadwort, i.e. the mead or honey-wine herb. The flowers are still used in beers and meads.

Salicylic acid was isolated from meadowsweet in the 1890s and used to make aspirin.

About Lady's Smock

Cardamine pratensis

"... Lady Smocks all silver white
and Cuckoo-buds of yellow hue
Do paint the meadows with delight"
William Shakespeare, *Love's Labours Lost*

Colloquial names:
*Cuckooflower, Milkmaids, Lucy Locket,
Mayflower, Meadowcress, Bread and Milk*

Where to find:
This lilac-pink flowerhead has clusters of
tiny flowers, which at times can fade to
white. As a child, if my parents asked where
I wanted to walk, I always replied Bowden
Hill, near Lacock in Wiltshire. On a clear day
you can see for miles and, in spring, if you
are lucky, you can hear the cuckoo and pick
lady's smock on the damp meadowland.
Unlike most flowers, it isn't sweet; in fact, it
is rather tangy. Less is more.

It grows in ditches, in our Angus garden,
and even in the cattle grid of my husband's
surgery in the Outer Hebrides, so lady's
smock, with its colorful red stem, had to be
included in this book (see *Wild Sourdough
Open Sandwiches*, page 53). The damper the
growing conditions, the taller the plant.

How to forage and gather:
Keep the flowers in water for as long
as possible, because they wilt quickly.
I'm interested that watercress is on a
"superfood" list and yet lady's smock, which
tastes quite similar, has been sidelined.
Possibly it is less prolific, or tricky to grow.

How to use:
Pick young, tender leaves and use sparingly
in salads and savory dishes. Both leaves and
flowers, which are exceedingly pretty, have
a warm, peppery taste.

Folklore:
The flower was named lady's smock in honor of the Virgin Mary, because it first comes into flower around Lady Day (The Feast of the Annunciation, March 25.) Another colloquial name, cuckooflower, equates with the blooming of the flower and the sound of the first cuckoo. In the 18th century, sailors ate lady's smock to combat scurvy, because it's high in vitamin C. This is why I'm left wondering why lady's smock isn't on the superfood list. It must contain starch, too, because in Elizabethan times, the plants were used to stiffen ruffles.

Wild Notes

A drizzle of Ramps (Wild Garlic) Oil, page 140, will add flavor and color contrast to the mauve of the lady's smock.

Cooked mussels can replace the bacon: omit the nettles and replace with shredded sorrel leaves. In fall, use wild mushrooms instead of bacon.

To every flower there is a season and when lady's smock fades, use bitter vetch instead. In fall, add seeds for extra crunch. I suggest using hogweed, gorse, sweet cicely (sparingly), and the tiny, black wild garlic seeds.

Wild SOURDOUGH open sandwiches

Serves 8

What to forage and find:
* 4 slices (rashers) bacon
* ¼ stick (25g) butter
* 2 good handfuls (50g) young nettle tops, washed
* 12 young sorrel stalks
* 12 lady's smock stalks (purple part only)
* 6–8 pickled ramps (wild garlic) stalks (optional)
* 4 tablespoons crème fraîche
* 5 oz (150g) blue cheese
* 4 thick slices of sourdough bread
* 16 lady's smock flowers, (optional)

What to do:
1 Preheat the broiler (grill) to high. Broil the bacon and use scissors to cut into small pieces. Set the bacon pieces to one side. Leave the broiler on.

2 Put any bacon fat and the butter in a skillet (frying pan) over low heat to melt the butter. Add the nettles and cook to wilt, 3–4 minutes.

3 Finely chop the sorrel and lady's smock stalks, add them to the wilted nettles, and cook briefly or the sorrel will discolor. Turn into a bowl to cool.

4 Shake the pickled ramps well to remove excess vinegar, and add them with the crème fraîche to the bowl. Crumble the cheese into the bowl, add the bacon, and stir gently to mix.

5 Lightly toast the sourdough bread on both sides, then top with the cheese mixture.

6 Broil (grill) for 3–4 minutes until the cheese bubbles and begins to brown.

7 Scatter the lady's smock flowers over the sandwiches and eat as soon as possible.

Flowers & Blossom

About Lime

Tilia vulgaris

"… presently my aunt would dip a little madeleine in the boiling infusion, whose taste of dead leaves or faded blossom she so relished, and hand me a piece when it was sufficiently soft."
Marcel Proust, *Du côté de chez Swann* (1913)

Colloquial names:
Linden, basswood, American linden trees, linn flowers

Where to find:
If you chance upon an avenue of lime (linden) trees on a hot sunny day in midsummer, the heady, honeyed scent of

linden blossom is intoxicating. As a child, I attended a school where collecting parents waited under shady lime trees. The small, fragrant, creamy yellow-green blossoms are my earliest memories of tree, rather than flower blossom and perfume. It's interesting how smell can trigger the waterfall of childhood memories. I also remember insects, lots of them, attracted to the trees' blossoms. Many lime trees have been planted in parkland; they have a rather majestic presence.

How to forage and gather:
Cut the linden blossom with scissors, or pull gently with finger and thumb, when the sun is out, and the flowers are in full bloom. Nature is clever—just as the elderflowers begin to fade, the linden blossoms and meadowsweet come into bloom.

How to use:
Linden tea is made from dried linden blossom. The blossom can be dried in a food dehydrator or on a sunny windowsill over two to three weeks. Once dry, store in an airtight container.

Fresh or dried linden blossom can be used when cooking fish (poaching liquid) or try it in *Couscous and Chicken infused with Linden*, opposite. The leaves can be eaten in salads, or as Richard Mabey suggests, sandwiches. In France, *Tilleul* (linden blossom) is used for tisanes, as the memorable quotation by Marcel Proust demonstrates. Honey made from linden blossom is of great value. The infused blossom will deliciously flavor syrups and cordials, which can be used in desserts, such as panna cotta (*Wild Cherry Blossom Panna Cotta*, page 41), sorbets, or ice cream; or use it in jellies such as *Crab Apple and Wild Honeysuckle Jelly*, page 115.

COUSCOUS and CHICKEN infused with *Linden*

This recipe can be adapted to use rose petals. Add a teaspoon of harissa paste to the rose chicken stock, and rose instead of linden blossom vinegar.

What to do:

1 Put the chicken breasts into a saucepan with the first bag of linden blossoms and enough water to cover. Bring the pan to a boil, cover with a lid, and simmer to poach the chicken (12–15 minutes). The chicken is cooked when the juices run clear when tested with a skewer. Remove the chicken to a plate to cool.

2 Put the chicken poaching liquid into a saucepan with the second bag of linden blossoms, cover, and simmer over very low heat for at least 20 minutes to infuse the linden. Allow to cool and remove the linden blossom sacks.

3 Wash, chop, and finely dice the cucumber, and put it into a sieve over a bowl. Sprinkle with salt and leave for 30 minutes, then rinse under running water and drain very well to remove excess water.

4 Rehydrate the couscous (adding liquid in accordance with the manufacturer's instructions). Put the couscous into a bowl and pour over the boiling, linden-blossom-infused chicken stock. Cover with plastic wrap (clingfilm) until the stock has been absorbed. Fluff up with a fork.

5 Cut the poached chicken into thin slices and add it with the cucumber, finely chopped parsley, and avocado chunks to the couscous.

6 Mix the linden blossom vinegar and olive oil together, season to taste, and pour over the couscous. Gently mix the ingredients together.

7 Turn into a serving dish and scatter with the toasted almonds.

Serves 4

What to forage and find:
For the chicken:
* 2 boneless, skinless chicken breasts, about 9 oz (250g)
* Handful of linden (lime) blossoms, wrapped and tied in a cheesecloth (muslin) bag
* Freshly ground black pepper
* Approximately 2½ cups (600ml) water

For the couscous:
* Scant cup (200ml) chicken poaching liquid (see *Wild Notes*, below)
* Handful of linden (lime) blossoms, wrapped and tied in a cheesecloth (muslin) bag
* 1 small cucumber
* Scant 1¼ cups (200g) whole-wheat (whole-grain) instant couscous
* Sea salt
* 1¼ cups (50g) finely chopped flat leaf parsley
* 1 ripe avocado, roughly chopped
* 1 tablespoon linden blossom (or rice) vinegar
* 2 tablespoons olive oil
* Freshly ground black pepper
* ¼ cup (25g) slivered (flaked) almonds, toasted

Wild Notes

For a more intense linden-blossom flavor, prepare the poaching liquid in advance by pouring boiling water over the blossoms, leaving it to steep overnight, straining the liquid into a pan, and then adding fresh blossoms. You can repeat the number of macerations until you achieve the desired linden-blossom flavor.

If you are using traditional (not instant) couscous, steam it over water and linden blossom (in cheesecloth). Add the chicken to the water for the final 10–15 minutes of cooking time, depending on the size of the chicken breasts.

Use a handful of linden blossoms in homemade madeleines and linden blossom in syrup to make ice cream. Linden blossom can be dried for use throughout the year.

Flowers & Blossom

55

CHAPTER 2

WOODLAND *and* *Hedgerow*

About Douglas Fir

Pseudotsuga menziesii

"If you go into the woods today…
And to this day, you can see the hind legs
and the tail of the mouse sticking out
from the Douglas fir cone, where he is
still hiding from the fox."
Description of the Douglas Fir cone

Where to find:

Douglas fir isn't a true fir, hence its Latin
name; and is a native of the US. One of the
oldest Douglas firs in the UK is planted in
Scone Palace in Perthshire, Scotland. It was
brought to the UK in seed form from North
America by David Douglas in 1826 (David
Douglas was born in the village of Scone).
The cones are smaller than others and have
interesting, distinctive "tongues" that
protrude between the cone scales. These
are rather aptly described above—a mouse
diving for cover into the Douglas fir cone.
The flat, single needles are individually
attached to the stem.

How to forage and gather:

The Douglas fir grows to great heights, but
it is the tips of the Douglas fir that are of
interest to the forager. They are rich in
vitamins, and young tips are best. Use these
for *Douglas Fir Syrup*, page 60, and *Douglas
Fir Chocolate Pots*, opposite. Gently pull the
tips from the branches and take just a few
needles from each branch to ensure that the
tree is not damaged. If you are using fresh,
not dried, leaves, then wrap them in a damp
cloth, because they dry out quickly.

How to use:

The leaves can be frozen, dried, or used
fresh. I make pine-needle sugars, tisanes,
butter, vinegar, oil, syrup, and cordial, and tie
them in a bunch of *bouquet garni* to give
flavor to stews, soups, and rice. Blend finely-
ground Douglas Fir needles with

confectioner's (icing) sugar and sprinkle over
festive pastries. The *Douglas Fir Christmas
Tree Cookies*, page 60, are perfect for
hanging on the festive tree, which is often a
Douglas fir.

I grind Douglas fir needles as finely as
possible in a mortar and pestle (it's tricky
to do this in a blender unless you have a
large amount) and store the powder in an
airtight jar. Its aromatic flavor adds interest
to many dishes—I often add a pinch when a
recipe calls for rosemary. It's delicious in hot
chocolate, such as *Violet Drinking Chocolate*,
page 29, or in smoothies.

Douglas Fir CHOCOLATE pots

This is a very rich dessert, so don't be tempted to use large ramekins.
I use tiny French chocolate pots.

What to do:

1 Put the Douglas fir sprig and cream into a saucepan and scald it over low heat. Do not allow the cream to boil. Set aside for an hour to allow the flavor to infuse, then remove the sprig.

2 Put the chocolate into a food processor and pulse to break it into small pieces. Take care: the machine may need to be held in place.

3 Reheat the cream (do not allow it to boil). Slowly pour the hot cream into the food processor and pulse, ensuring that the chocolate doesn't overflow down the sides of the machine. If you don't chop the chocolate first, it may do this. So slowly does it.

4 Add the egg to the hot chocolate cream, blend, then add the Douglas Fir Syrup or pine sugar. Pour into pots and refrigerate until set.

Makes 6–8, depending on size

What to forage and find:

* Sprig of Douglas fir, approximately 2½–3 inches (6–8cm) in length, washed and dried
* 1¼ cups (300ml) light (single) cream
* 7 oz (200g) bittersweet (dark) chocolate (minimum 70% cocoa solids)
* 1 medium (small UK) egg
* 2 teaspoons *Douglas Fir Syrup* (page 60) or pine sugar (see *Blackberry and Wild Thyme Leathers*, page 15)

Wild Notes

You can adapt this easy chocolate pot recipe by replacing the Douglas fir with another wild herb, flower sugar, or syrup. Decorate with crystallized flowers if desired. Serve with Douglas Fir Christmas Tree Cookies, page 60.

Woodland & Hedgerow

Douglas Fir CHRISTMAS TREE cookies

An edible treat or a homemade Christmas tree decoration.

Makes 40

What to forage and find:
* dry Douglas fir needles
* 1¼ cups (125g) sifted confectioners' (icing) sugar
* 1¾ sticks (200g) butter, cut into small cubes
* 1 medium (small UK) egg yolk
* 2¼ cups (300g) all-purpose (plain) flour, plus extra for rolling
* Glacé icing and silver balls, to decorate (optional)

What to do:

1 Preheat the oven to 375°F (190°C/ gas mark 5).

2 Put the dry Douglas fir needles with the confectioners' (icing) sugar in a food processor. Cover with a kitchen (tea) towel (the dust seems to escape even when the lid is firmly on), and blend to chop the pine needles finely.

3 Add the butter and egg yolk to the food processor, and then enough flour to make dough. Wrap in plastic wrap (clingfilm), and refrigerate for at least an hour before using.

4 Lightly dust a work surface with flour, and roll out the pine dough. Stamp out thin ⅛-inch (3mm) Christmas trees with

a cookie cutter, place on a nonstick baking tray, and bake for approximately 8–10 minutes (depending on thickness). Check after 8 minutes—the trees will brown very suddenly. Cool for 2–3 minutes, then use a spatula to transfer the trees to a wire rack.

5 To hang the cookies on a Christmas tree: use a skewer to make a small hole in the dough of the Christmas tree (to thread ribbon through) before baking at step 4.

6 Decorate with glacé icing and silver balls if desired, or frame the trees with a small amount of icing.

Douglas Fir SYRUP

Splash into vodka or gin cocktails, or simply dilute with tonic water.

Makes about 1¾ cups (400ml)

What to forage and find:
* 1 cup (25g) Douglas fir or pine needles*
* Scant 1 cup (200ml) boiling water
* 2 cups (400g) superfine (caster) sugar

* Use Douglas fir, Scots pine, or other edible pine needles

What to do:

1 Put the pine needles in a large, sterilized jam jar (with a lid) and pour in the boiling water. Cover and leave for 24 hours.

2 Strain the pine-needle-infused water into a pitcher (jug).

3 Put the sugar in a clean saucepan and add the strained water. Heat over low heat to dissolve the sugar. DO NOT STIR.

4 Bring to a boil for 2–3 minutes until you have reached the desired consistency.

5 Leave to cool and then pour into a sterilized bottle and refrigerate. Use within a month.

Wild Notes

For greener syrup, add a tablespoon of washed and dried chickweed tops, after removing the boiled syrup from the heat (step 4). Blend in a food processor and strain again before bottling. As with all cordials and syrups, for best color, use refined sugar.

About Perennial Stinging Nettle

Urtica dioica

"The sting of the nettle is but nothing compared to the pain that it heals"
Lelord Kordel

Colloquial names:
Devil's Plaything, Devil's Leaf, Hokey-Pokey, Seven Minute Itch, Jenny-Nettle, Common Nettle

Where to find:
The leaves, which are rich in vitamins A and C, can be found almost everywhere: on roadsides, wastelands, in woods, and in meadows, by streams, grassy places, and in gardens.

How to forage and gather:
Nettles for consumption should be picked in early spring while young. The green leaves, which are oval with a pointy, heart-shaped base, are covered in tiny hairs. In later spring, use only the tips and young leaves. Don't pick beyond early summer, or after flowering. Wear rubber gloves when collecting nettle leaves for obvious reasons; "stingability" decreases as the nettle is cooked or dried. I'm told that if you harvest nettles after rain, the sting factor is zero. Richard Mabey describes how to eat nettles in their raw state: it involves quickly grasping the nettle by the stem, thereby crushing the hairs before they pierce the skin. It sounds like a schoolboy dare, and I have no desire to test this theory.

Nettles do, however, have their uses: the Germans, plagued by textile shortages in the First World War, used them instead of cotton to make uniforms, and folklore suggests that, when carried, they ward off evil spirits.

How to use:
Historically, nettles have been used in soups; there is a recipe for St Columba's broth, a 6th-century Irish recipe, and there are soup recipes by the ancient herbalists Culpepper and Gerard. A simple potato-based nettle soup is easy to cook. Follow the recipe for *Nettle Purée*, page 64, and simply add potato, onion, and stock. Nettles were also used cooked and puréed in desserts (even syllabubs), beers, and wine, and there is a current revival of nettle cordials and syrups.

Renewal of nettle interest is associated with times of economic hardship, an example being recipes in Ambrose Heath's *Kitchen Front Recipes and Hints* (1941), and there appears to be a current trend to eat them again. This could, however, be due to an increased popularity in foraging.

I use wilted nettles in place of spinach in egg-based dishes—quiches and frittatas. The leaves lend themselves to pesto. They are equally delicious either puréed or wilted, and mixed with root vegetables. The leaves can be steeped in vinegar to make nettle vinegar (see *Elderflower Vinegar*, page 18). Alternatively, they can be dried in a food dehydrator, and used for tea infusions, or sprinkled into savory crumble toppings. The young leaves can be juiced (see *Ramps [Wild Garlic] Oil*, page 140) and the juice frozen in ice cubes or other small containers.

SALMON and *Nettle* fishcakes

The nettles in the fishcakes will remain a vibrant green when cooked, giving a lovely pink and green color contrast. When cooked, nettles lose their sting.

What to do:

1 Put the fish, bay leaf, and peppercorns in a saucepan, and cover with the milk. Poach the fish on low heat until it is just cooked (3–4 minutes). Take the fish out of the pan with a slotted spoon, remove the skin, and roughly flake the fish into a bowl.

2 Cook the diced potatoes in the fish milk, taking care not to let the milk burn. When the potatoes are cooked (10–15 minutes), drain, and put them with the butter in the bowl with the fish. (Discard the bay leaf and peppercorns, and retain the milk for a fish sauce or soup.)

3 Meanwhile, steam the nettles for 3–4 minutes. Refresh under cold water, and use your hands to squeeze excess water from the nettles before adding

them to the bowl. Season with nutmeg and pepper, and mash everything together. Leave to cool.

4 Make 4–6 fishcakes and put them on a tray in the fridge for 10 minutes.

5 Put the flour, beaten egg, and breadcrumbs on separate plates and dip the fishcakes first in the flour, then the egg, and finally the breadcrumbs. Return to the fridge for 30 minutes, or longer if possible, to allow the fishcakes to firm up.

6 Heat a tablespoon of oil and knob of butter in a skillet (frying pan) and cook the fishcakes for 4–5 minutes on each side until golden brown, replenishing the butter and oil as necessary.

Serves 4–6

What to forage and find:
* 9 oz (250g) fresh salmon fillet
* Fresh bay leaf
* 2 peppercorns
* 1¼ cups (300ml) milk
* Scant 1 lb (400g) potatoes, peeled and diced
* Knob of butter
* 1½ large handfuls (75g) nettle leaves
* Freshly grated nutmeg
* Freshly ground black pepper
* 4 tablespoons (30g) all-purpose (plain) flour
* 1 egg, beaten
* About ½ cup (50g) breadcrumbs
* Butter and oil for cooking

Wild Notes

You may prefer to coat the fishcakes with rolled oats instead of breadcrumbs.

In early spring, replace the nettles with young hawthorn leaves, or if you live by the sea, try cooked laver (seaweed).

Woodland & Hedgerow

POACHED EGGS and *Nettle Purée*

Serve this simple breakfast or supper dish with smoked salmon on special occasions.

Serves 4

What to forage and find:
* 1 recipe quantity *Nettle Purée*, see below
* 4 extra large (large UK) eggs
* 2 English muffins, cut in half and lightly toasted
* Butter for the muffins
* Finely ground sea lettuce or freshly ground black pepper

What to do:
1 Make the nettle purée (see below).

2 Fill a skillet (frying pan) three-quarters full with water and bring to a boil.

3 Break an egg into a small bowl and turn the heat up so that the water in the pan boils vigorously. Drop the egg into the center of the pan, reduce the temperature, and simmer for 2–3 minutes, until the egg white and yolk are just set. Remove the poached egg with a slotted spoon, and repeat to cook all of the eggs. (I am happy to poach two eggs at a time, but no more.)

4 Lightly butter the muffins and put them on four plates. Divide the nettle purée between the muffins, and put a poached egg on top of the nettle purée. Sprinkle a little finely ground sea lettuce (or ground pepper) on the egg yolk and serve immediately.

Nettle Purée

Some recipes add milk to nettles to make the purée, but I find milk and nettles separate on reheating. Mixing blanched nettles with a thick white sauce gives the best results. I also like adding this thick, vibrant green nettle purée to mashed potato or to quiches.

Serves 4

What to forage and find:
* 3 good handfuls (75g) nettle tips
* ¼ stick (25g) butter
* 3 tablespoons (25g) all-purpose (plain) flour
* 1¼ cups (300ml) milk
* Sea salt and freshly ground black pepper
* Freshly grated nutmeg

What to do:
1 Blanch the nettles in salted water for 2 minutes, drain, then refresh in ice water. This will ensure the purée remains green.

2 Wring the water from the nettles with your hands (cooking takes away the sting) to remove as much water as you can. It is very important to get the nettles as dry as possible. You could spin them in a salad spinner.

3 Make a simple white sauce: melt the butter in a saucepan over low heat, and beat in the flour to make a roux. Slowly add the cold milk, whisking continuously until the sauce has thickened.

4 Season with salt and pepper, and add a large pinch of freshly grated nutmeg. Bring the sauce to a boil, and simmer for 5–6 minutes, stirring frequently.

5 Whiz the blanched nettles and sauce in a food processor until you have a thick, smooth purée. Return to the pan and heat through. Serve immediately.

Wild Notes

Add extra blanched nettles, milk, or cream to make a thinner nettle sauce (pouring consistency).

Add hot nettle purée to 1¼ lb (600g) of warm, cooked, and well-drained potatoes for wild green mash.

Serves 6

What to forage and find:

For the pesto:
* 2 good handfuls (50g) young nettle leaves
* Handful of ramps (wild garlic), washed, or 1 clove garlic, chopped
* ¼ cup (25g) grated Parmesan cheese
* ¼ cup (25g) toasted pine nuts
* Freshly ground black pepper
* Juice of ½ small lime
* About ½ cup (100ml) olive oil

For the pie:
* ¼ stick (25g) butter, plus extra for greasing
* Large leek, washed and finely shredded
* 2 tablespoons *nettle pesto* (see above)
* 14–15 cherry tomatoes, halved
* 1 cup (125g) mozzarella cheese, cut into ½-inch (1cm) cubes
* 9 oz (250g) puff pastry
* Flour for rolling
* 3 black olives, finely chopped

Frugal and tasty, this dish brightens up the table, and can be adapted to use other wild leaves and pestos as the seasons pass by.

LADYBIRDS in *Wild Pesto*

What to do:

1 Boil the nettles for 1 minute, drain, and plunge in iced water. Remove when cold and squeeze them as dry as you can. To make the pesto, put the nettles and all the other ingredients apart from the oil in a food processor and blend. With the machine running slowly, add enough oil to make a thick paste.

2 Preheat the oven to 425°F (220°C/ gas mark 7). Grease a 5½ x 7-inch (14 x 18cm) shallow ovenproof dish.

3 Heat the butter in a skillet (frying pan) and add the shredded leeks. Cook for 2–3 minutes, but do not allow them to

brown. Remove the pan from the heat, add the pesto, and stir well.

4 Put the cherry tomato halves, skin side down in the greased dish. Scatter the mozzarella and evenly spread the leeks and pesto over the top.

5 Roll the pastry to roughly fit the dish and place over the mixture. Turn the edges in to make the pastry fit the dish.

6 Bake for 15–20 minutes until the pastry is golden. Leave to cool for 2–3 minutes. Turn the dish upside down over a serving dish and decorate the tomatoes with chopped olives to resemble ladybug (ladybird) spots.

SPRING *Nettle* parcels

These wild parcels are delicious hot, and cold they are easily carried for picnics and school or office lunches.

Makes 4

What to forage and find:
* 2 cups (100g) young nettle leaves
* ¼ stick (25g) butter
* 2 medium leeks, washed and finely chopped
* 1½–2 cups (100g) small mushrooms, washed and thinly sliced
* 2 tablespoons toasted pine nuts
* 5 oz (150g) feta cheese
* 8 sheets phyllo (filo) pastry, 6 x 6 inches (15 x 15cm)
* About ¾ stick (75g) butter, melted

What to do:
1 Preheat the oven to 375°F (190°C/gas mark 5).

2 Prepare the filling. Rinse the nettles well, and steam for 3–4 minutes. Squeeze any excess water from the leaves, then put them into a bowl and set aside.

3 Melt 1 tablespoon (15g) butter over low heat and cook the leeks for 3–4 minutes, stirring continuously. Add the leeks to the nettles.

4 Heat 2 teaspoons (10g) butter and sauté the mushrooms briefly. Add to the nettles and leeks.

5 Add the toasted pine nuts, and crumble the cheese into the bowl.

6 Trim the phyllo pastry sheet as necessary. For each parcel, brush a square of pastry with melted butter before layering a second square on top. Brush with butter again, and place one quarter of the prepared filling in the center of the pastry. Pull the four corners together, and twist into a pouch. Brush the parcel with melted butter. Hold the parcel firmly in one hand, brush the base with butter, and put it onto a baking sheet lined with parchment paper. Work quickly to prepare the remaining three parcels—phyllo pastry dries out very quickly.

7 Bake for about 15 minutes, until the parcels are golden.

8 Eat immediately with a lightly tossed salad, or a tomato sauce, or nettle purée in white sauce. (See *Poached Eggs and Nettle Purée*, page 64.)

Wild Notes

Ramps (wild garlic) are in season with young nettles, so they could be added for a more garlicky taste. I, however, prefer to savor the flavor of spring nettles, which can be lost in the garlic. In the fall, adapt this recipe to use wild mushrooms and a cornucopia of wild seeds. For an added garlic kick, use Ramps (Wild Garlic) Oil, page 140, to sauté the leeks and mushrooms.

For a lower saturated fat content, brush the phyllo pastry with olive oil instead of butter.

Woodland & Hedgerow

67

About Hazelnut

Corylus avellana

Colloquial names:
Lamb's Tails, Catkin, Cobnut, Witch Hazel, Wood Nut, Filbert

Where to find:
The small hazelnut tree, found in woodlands and hedgerows, also flourishes well on chalky land. It bears fruit in late summer until mid-fall. In spring, the male yellow catkins (lambs' tails) are a sight to behold, but the tiny, red female flower is needed, too.

How to forage and gather:
Squirrels will usually get to hazelnuts before they ripen. If you fare better than I do, here's what to do.

Gather hazelnuts after a spell of fine weather, so that the outer husks aren't damp. Lay them on trays lined with newspaper, and store them somewhere warm for two weeks, turning them as often as you can remember. Remove the husks and store the hazelnuts in their shells. As with all wild nuts, they need plenty of circulating air or they will go moldy. This is important if you have gathered them after a period of wet weather.

To roast hazelnuts, spread the shelled nuts on a baking sheet and bake at 275°F (130°C/gas mark 1) for 20 minutes. Alternatively, you can dry-roast the hazelnuts in a skillet (frying pan) on the stovetop (hob), turning frequently, until the skins have cracked. Put the roasted hazelnuts in a clean, damp kitchen (tea) towel, and rub with vigor until the skins come away.

How to use:
Nuts add texture, as well as being a rich source of proteins, oils, and fats. I add finely chopped or ground hazelnuts to bread, baking, and sweet and savory crumbles. They are also useful in cereal, blitzed in fruit smoothies, or in salads.

Folklore:
The nuts are said to ripen on August 20, the Feast of St Philibert; the hazelnut, also called a filbert, is said to have been named after him.

The Brothers Grimm fairy tales suggest that the hazel gives protection from venomous things, while Druid legend says that the person who dines on salmon fed on hazelnuts will be wise. You might try them with Brussels sprouts on Christmas day.

Wild Hazelnut and chocolate ice-cream pops

Our younger three children were affectionately known as the "Trashers" due to the trail of debris they left after a meal. The chocolate-loving trio tried this recipe many times until eventually they gave it the thumbs up.

What to do:

1 Put the hazelnut spread, milk, and cream in a saucepan, and cook over low heat to melt. Whisk well to ensure that there aren't any chocolate lumps on the base of the pan. Allow the mixture to cool and stir well (the hazelnuts will rise to the top).

2 Pour into prepared ice-cream pop (ice lolly) molds (washed fromage frais pots work well, too), and freeze. When the mixture is slushy, stir well to redistribute the nuts. Freeze until frozen solid.

Makes 4–6, depending on size

What to forage and find:
* 3 tablespoons *Wild Hazelnut and Chocolate Spread*, page 70
* 1 scant cup (200ml) whole milk
* Scant ½ cup (100ml) heavy (double) cream

Wild Notes

If using homemade containers: halfway through the freezing time, when the mixture is slushy, gently push a lollipop stick into the container.

Dip the molds in hot water to loosen the ice-cream pops, and enjoy them as soon as possible.

Wild Hazelnut and chocolate spread

Give the hazelnuts and sugar a wild whiz in a food processor and the rest is easy. Once you've made this delicious chocolate spread you won't ever buy another supermarket jar.

Makes 1 small bowl

What to forage and find:
* ⅜ cup (50g) hazelnuts
* Heaping ½ cup (50g) sifted confectioners' (icing) sugar
* 3½ oz (100g) milk chocolate
* 3 generous tablespoons heavy (double) cream
* 1 teaspoon hazelnut oil
* About 1 tablespoon vegetable oil

What to do:
1 Blend the hazelnuts and confectioners' (icing) sugar in a food processor until it is your desired spread texture.

2 Break the chocolate into a heat-resistant bowl that fits snugly over a pan of simmering water. When the chocolate begins to melt, add the cream and the blended nuts and sugar. Stir continuously until the chocolate has melted into the crushed nuts.

3 Add the hazelnut and canola (vegetable) oils to bind the mixture—it will become firmer when cold.

4 Stir well, and leave to cool before using in cake fillings, or on toasted sourdough bread.

5 Make as needed. Do not refrigerate, or the chocolate will harden.

Wild Notes

Add a teaspoon of wild hazelnut chocolate spread to smoothies or hot chocolate. Use bittersweet chocolate for grown-ups. Try using roasted chestnuts or walnuts instead of hazelnuts.

This sticky shortbread rarely lasts long in our house—my children, like squirrels, love hazelnuts. Sometimes I adapt this recipe by replacing the sea salt with a teaspoon of dried sea lettuce.

Salted CARAMEL *Wild Hazelnut* shortbread

What to do:

1 Preheat the oven to 300°F (150°C/gas mark 2).

2 To make the shortbread, mix the butter, sugar, and flour together in a bowl until they form a dough. Press the dough into an 8-inch (20cm) cake pan (tin) lined with parchment paper.

3 Chop the hazelnuts and sea salt in a food processor and scatter the hazelnuts over the shortbread dough. Push the nuts down into the dough and bake for 35 minutes, until the dough is firm, but not colored. Leave the shortbread to cool.

4 To make the caramel layer, put the caramel ingredients in a saucepan, and cook over low heat, stirring continuously, until the butter and sugar have melted, and the caramel has thickened (about 5 minutes).

5 Pour the caramel over the hazelnut shortbread and leave to set.

6 To make the frosting (icing), melt the chocolate and butter in a bowl over a pan of simmering water, then pour the mixture over the set caramel. Leave the chocolate to set, and cut into small slices.

Wild Notes

Use wild thyme sugar in place of superfine (caster) sugar in the shortbread. Coastal foragers can replace caramel with Sea Lettuce and Caramel Sauce, page 165.

Makes 10 slices of rich deliciousness

What to forage and find:

For the shortbread:
* 1 scant stick (100g) salted butter
* ¼ cup (50g) superfine (caster) sugar
* 1⅛ cups (150g) all-purpose (plain) flour
* 1⅛ cups (150g) roasted hazelnuts
* 1 teaspoon sea salt

For the caramel:
* 1 scant stick (100g) salted butter
* ½ cup (100g) light brown sugar
* 4 tablespoons condensed milk

For the frosting (icing):
* 7 oz (200g) bittersweet (dark) chocolate, minimum 70% cocoa solids
* ¼ stick (25g) salted butter

Woodland & Hedgerow

73

About Fungi

Antonio Carluccio begins his introduction to *A Passion For Mushrooms* with: "Everything about wild mushrooms is a pleasure to me." If only others, including some foragers, felt this way. Many wild food gatherers neglect the mushroom because they are fearful.

My mushroom education came on in leaps and bounds one summer, when Stephanie Monce, a French *au pair*, came to help with the children. She dragged our older children and me up hills and through wooded glens, and taught me to confidently identify chanterelles, ceps, puffballs, hen of the woods, boletus, and more. I have not looked back. A little foraging time spent in the company of an expert, and the knowledge is with you for life. However, with fungi, always err on the side of caution—if you are *in any doubt, don't pick it*. Thanks to Stephanie, our six children can sniff out edible wild fungi with confidence.

There is much controversy over eating foraged mushrooms, and you should certainly only forage with experience, or help from someone who has it, and carefully check your hoard when you return home. This said, the number of screwed-up noses I receive when I say that I've been picking wild mushrooms interests me: perhaps it is because some look unappetizing, or because some of them look rather rude (young ceps). Who knows, but for my part, I stick closely to mushrooms that I can safely identify, and find yummy to eat. A rich source of protein, their addition will delight a vegetarian who is aiming for a nutritionally balanced plate.

The following is not an extensive guide to mushrooms but a brief guide to my favorites.

Chanterelle
Cantharellus cibarius

Colloquial name:
Girolles

Where to find:
In woodlands, especially under beech and pine trees. Once you have found chanterelles, mark the spot—they return each year from midsummer to early fall.

How to forage and gather:
In one wood I visit, chanterelles carpet the ground and foraging is easy, but this is when you must not be greedy. The orange cap is flattish, often dipped in the center. The thick, orange ridges on the cap's underside run down the orange stem, and it has the aroma of apricot. Beware of the aptly named "false chanterelle," which has thin, unridged gills. In America, there is a blue chanterelle—a magnificent color contrast.

How to use:
Eat them sautéed in butter or in egg or pasta dishes. You may like to dry chanterelles and use them out of season. Dried and finely ground mushrooms are useful in stock, risottos, and casseroles.

Folklore:
"When the moon is in the full, mushrooms you may freely pull. But when the moon is on the wane, wait ere you think to pluck again."

Another old wives' tale suggests that if fungi look good, they are edible—no wonder folk are wary of foraging for mushrooms.

Common Puffball
Lycoperdon perlatum

Colloquial names:
Poukball, Puck-fish

Where to find:
In woods from early summer to early winter, and on badly tended golf courses.

How to forage and gather:
Young puffballs are white and club-shaped but brown with age. Pick them white, or pale, and about 1¼–1½ inches (3–4 cm) in size. Older ones become powdery. Do not confuse with the common earthball, a poisonous mushroom—on maturity the flesh turns black.

How to use:
Cook as quickly as possible. They have a meat-like texture and can be sliced or cubed and sautéed in butter or added to stews, casseroles, or soup. A layer in vegetarian lasagna works well, too.

Some foraging tips:
Chanterelles are well suited to my Angus neighborhood; they enjoy the combination of warmth and dampness. Maxim, our youngest son, has been chanterelle hunting since he was a toddler; his rain (wellington) boots have fallen into muddy streams (chanterelles hide under moss and bracken on the banks of ditches), but nowadays, he's usually way ahead of me in the woods, on his mission to find those orange mushrooms that smell so delicately of apricots—in "Chanterelle Heaven." We call it heaven because, on finding one chanterelle, more will soon turn up; they lurk in the undergrowth disguised as fallen beech leaves. Our take-home message for take-home heaven is:

* Ask the landowner's permission before you help yourself. Mushrooms are a contradiction: considered peasants' food, landowners are well aware that high-class restaurants pay large sums of money for foraged fungi.

* Don't forage by busy roads. Field mushrooms often grow on the edge of roads, but don't be tempted by the often large, but car-polluted, fungus.

* Pick only for your supper pot, not your neighbor's, i.e. forage sustainably.

* Use a basket (not a plastic bag), because fungi decay quickly, and need to be kept cool and aerated.

* Use a knife. There is a special mushroom knife called an "Opinel"—it's French, of course; that nation is full of wild mushroom lovers. If the mycelium (a fine net of threads at the mushroom base) is broken, this may prevent future growth.

* Take care that maggots aren't spoiling the mushrooms — give the fungi a good brush before eating. You can buy a special brush for this purpose. I don't wash mushrooms.

* Invest in a mushroom guide.

* If this is your first tasting, don't be greedy, just in case the mushrooms don't agree with you.

Giant Puffball
Calvatia gigantea (previously classified as *Lycoperdon giganteum*)

Colloquial names:
Giant Gem Studded, Pear-Shaped Puffball

Where to find:
At the edge of fields, in ditches, on wasteland, in woodland, and on banked hedgerows. I call it a "groupie" because if you spy one, on closer inspection there will usually be a friend or two hanging around.

How to forage and gather:
Gather them from late summer to early fall. Specimens should be firm and the flesh white, not yellowing. Make sure they are maggot-free.

How to use:
Use as the common puffball.

Bolete
Boletus edulis

Colloquial names:
Cep, Penny Bun

Where to find:
You can identify the boletus family by their spongy gills. They are often found in twos and threes in deciduous woods, especially near beech trees, from early summer to late fall. They are easily identified by their spongy undersides. The brown cap darkens as it gets bigger.

How to forage and gather:
Gatherers should cut larger (older) specimens in half to check for maggots. Antonio Carluccio says that the cep should be twisted, not cut with a knife, because "there is danger … that the part left in the ground will eventually rot and destroy the mycelium, preventing further fruit." The penny bun is, in my opinion, the very quintessence of fungi —earthy and rich—and when I find one, my heart misses a beat, but it is a rarity.

Field Mushroom
Agaricus campestris

Colloquial names:
Pink Bottoms, Meadow Mushroom

How to forage and gather:
From late summer to mid-fall, in open fields (note that *campus* is Latin for field), on grassy edges of roads; perhaps this is one reason why many people are happy to forage this shop-familiar mushroom rather than those of woodland habitat. Field mushrooms often grow near horse and cow manure, so forage (with livestock care) in grazing meadows. Train your eye and as with all foraging, you will soon spot mushrooms everywhere. The pink gills of field mushrooms darken with age. Youthful specimens may be eaten raw and older ones are excellent in mushroom ketchup.

How to use:
I don't wash or peel mushrooms, but I do open older ones to check for maggots. I rarely dry mushrooms, but have visited kitchens where whole and sliced chanterelles and ceps are hanging out to dry with the family washing on a Sheila Pulley Maid (a famous UK ceiling-hung airing rack) above a range stove. Store in a sealed jam jar.

To freeze mushrooms, wipe (don't peel) and flash (open-freeze) until frozen. Then tightly pack the fungi in a rigid container, label, and store in the freezer. For best results, cook from frozen in melted butter. Wild mushrooms can be frozen in prepared dishes, too.

TOP TO BOTTOM:
Giant puffball, bolete, field mushroom

This is a recipe to cook with family and friends—you can easily increase the quantities and use whichever edible mushrooms you can find when foraging. Cooks can take turns in stirring the pot, but take care not to overcook the rice.

Foragers' AUTUMN RISOTTO

Serves 4

What to forage and find:
* 3 tablespoons (40g) butter
* 1 tablespoon olive oil
* Small red onion, finely diced
* 1 clove garlic, finely chopped
* 1 teaspoon wild thyme leaves
* Generous 1½ cups (300g) risotto rice
* Scant ¼ cup (50ml) white wine
* About 4 cups (1 liter) warm vegetable (or dried mushroom) stock
* 1 tablespoon cream cheese
* 1½ cups (100g) chanterelles, or other wild fungi, wiped clean and roughly sliced
* 1 tablespoon toasted pine nuts
* 2 tablespoons chopped chickweed
* Freshly ground black pepper

What to do:
1 Heat half the butter and the oil in a large, shallow pan and soften the onion over low heat. Do not allow the onion to brown.

2 Add the garlic, thyme, and rice, and stir with a wooden spoon, to coat the rice with the oil.

3 Add the wine. When the wine is absorbed, gradually add the warm stock, a ladleful at a time. Continue stirring and adding the stock, ladle by ladle, until it has all been absorbed and the rice is cooked, about 15–20 minutes.

4 Stir in the cream cheese, and remove the pan from the heat.

5 Meanwhile, heat the remaining butter in a skillet (frying pan) and cook the mushrooms for 1–2 minutes.

6 Gently stir the mushrooms, toasted pine nuts, and chopped chickweed into the risotto, season with black pepper, and eat as soon as possible.

Wild Notes

Use fruit vinegars instead of the wine. Blackberry vinegar would be delicious and seasonal.

Seashore mussels, razor clams, or clams (cockles) could be used instead of, or in addition to, wild fungi. Discard any open shells before cooking: heat a little olive oil and crushed garlic in a pan, add the grit-free and de-bearded (as required) shellfish, and wait for the molluscs to open (1–2 minutes), then add the cooked shellfish and their juices to the risotto. Serve sprinkled with toasted wild seeds.

Woodland & Hedgerow

GRIDDLED *Field Mushrooms*

Field mushrooms should be eaten as soon as possible and this is often at breakfast time in our house. But with a little preparation beforehand, they make a nutritious supper—mushrooms are protein and mineral rich.

Makes 4

What to forage and find:
* 1 tablespoon *Blackberry and Wild Water Mint Vinegar*, page 93
* 2 tablespoons olive oil
* 2 tablespoons chopped parsley
* 1 tablespoon wild thyme leaves
* Sea salt and freshly ground black pepper
* 4 large field mushrooms, wiped clean
* Crusty bread, to serve

What to do:
1 Mix the blackberry vinegar, canola (olive) oil, herbs, and seasoning in a small bowl.

2 Put the wiped mushrooms into a large plastic bag and carefully pour the marinade into the bag. Seal the bag, and leave for an hour.

3 Griddle the mushrooms or broil (grill) for 3–4 minutes on each side.

4 Slice, and serve warm with bread to mop up the juices.

Wild Notes
Melt some wild herb or seaweed butter on the griddle and cook the mushrooms cap side down. Griddle over low heat and, as the mushrooms cook, fill them with more butter, adding additional freshly chopped herbs or fresh or rehydrated seaweed. Alternatively, toss the mushrooms in egg and seaweed breadcrumbs, and cook in melted dulse or sea lettuce butter in a skillet (frying pan). See Seaweed and Butternut Squash Cakes, page 174.

Poached *Wild Mushroom* mini QUICHES

Poaching mushrooms is a healthier cooking method than sautéing them in butter prior to baking. Add flowers with the wild thyme to enhance presentation. Mini quiches are easy-peasy to serve, and, when cold, they are useful in lunch boxes.

What to do:

1 Preheat the oven to 400°F (200°C/gas mark 6).

2 Rub the flours and fats together until the mixture resembles breadcrumbs, and add enough water or stock to make a dough.

3 Lightly grease 5 individual flan dishes. Roll the pastry thinly and line the greased dishes. Prick each base a few times with a fork. Cover the pastry with aluminum foil and baking beans, and bake blind for 7–8 minutes.

4 Remove the foil and beans, and return the pastry to the oven for about 3 minutes to crisp the base. The cases are now ready for the filling. Reduce the oven temperature to 300°F (150°C/gas mark 2).

5 Meanwhile, put the sliced mushrooms in a saucepan, and add enough stock to cover. Bring to a boil, and simmer for 3–4 minutes. Drain, and pat the mushrooms dry with paper towels (kitchen paper).

6 Break the eggs into a bowl, add the cream and seasoning, and whisk well.

7 Pop the cooked pastry cases on a baking tray and divide the mushrooms between them. Pour the egg mixture over the mushrooms. Scatter the wild thyme over the top.

8 Bake until the quiches are just set (about 10–12 minutes). Remove the quiches from the oven and leave them to cool and continue setting.

Makes 5 individual shallow 4-inch (10cm) quiches

What to forage and find:
For the pastry:
* 6 tablespoons (50g) all-purpose (plain) flour
* Heaping ⅓ cup (50g) seeded whole-wheat (wholemeal) bread flour
* 2 scant tablespoons (25g) lard
* 2 scant tablespoons (25g) butter
* 2–3 tablespoons iced water or mushroom stock
* Butter to grease

For the filling:
* 1 generous cup (75g) cleaned and roughly sliced chanterelles and ceps
* Vegetable or mushroom stock or wild herb infusion (see *Wild Notes*, left)
* 2 extra large (large UK) eggs
* Scant ½ cup (100ml) light (single) cream
* Sea salt and freshly ground black pepper
* 1 tablespoon wild thyme leaves

Wild Notes

If you have time: add wild herbs—thyme and marjoram—with a bay leaf and a slice of lemon to 3 cups (750ml) boiling water and leave for a couple of hours to cool and allow the flavors to infuse.

Older chanterelles can sometimes be tough, but poaching will soften them.

Woodland & Hedgerow

About Chickweed

Stellaria media

"The Democrats are the party of government activism; the party that says government can make you richer, smarter, taller, and get the chickweed out of your lawn."
P. J. O'Rourke

Colloquial names:
Starweed, Starwort, Satin Flower, Tongue Grass, Winterweed, Chicken's Meat, Chickenweed

Where to find:
On uncultivated or wild land, chickweed pops up all over the place. It also appears in badly tended window boxes, and will carpet the lazy gardener's beds, so it can be picked in handfuls with a clear conscience. It grows with abundance on wasteland, footpaths, and roadsides, and chokes crops in fields.

Chickweed has naturalized itself where man has settled, and is a common weed. It has a sprawling, trailing habit with green, oval leaves, tiny, white, star-shaped flowers, and is the bane of a neat gardener's life. Its five flower petals divide, so it looks as though it has 10 petals. The flowers can bloom in very early spring and continue into late fall. There are tiny hairs on the stem, which change sides at each leaf junction. Mouse-ear chickweed has more hairs and won't harm you, but as my son, Jhonti, said, "The eating experience isn't pleasurable."

How to forage and gather:
If the weather is mild, chickweed can be picked throughout the year, although the spring leaves are best. Wild birds and domesticated hens enjoy it, as do pigs and rabbits, although our local garden rabbits aren't doing a very good job of keeping it at bay. It is often the only fresh green available in winter, and as such, is useful to the wild cook. The late summer leaves are best avoided.

I use scissors to cut chickweed; this makes it easier to prepare (the muddy roots come away easily, if you tug at it). The lower stems can be stringy, so I suggest cutting high, using the young stems from the top of the plant.

How to use:
Chickweed has a subtle mild flavor, so there is no need to hold back. It can be used in sandwiches, salads, dips, and pesto. Add it to omelets and sauces at the last minute to avoid overcooking. When cooked, its volume is greatly reduced—rather like spinach. Steaming, or wilting in a stir-fry, are my favorite cooking methods.

Folklore:
Chickweed is a weather barometer. Its leaves fold when there is rain about, but it isn't an early riser—its flowers don't open until late morning. In lean times, it was used in bread and to thicken soups.

Chickweed's colloquial names starweed or starwort are associated with its star-like flowers. But I've often wondered if it's called chickweed because hens love it—ours certainly do.

Chickweed water is an old wives' remedy for obesity. I'm trying this out, but suspect that overindulging in Violet Macarons with Primrose Cream, page 33, is where my problem may lie.

If time is on your side, make a tempura (see page 131) and deep-fry the puffball slices. If you pan fry, do it carefully—the puffball slices will absorb oil and butter and can become soggy.

Pan-fried *Puffball* with Carrot and Cardamom Purée

Serves 4

What to forage and find:
* ✳ 4 cardamom pods
* ✳ 18 oz (500g) carrots
* ✳ Juice of 1 orange
* ✳ About 2 teaspoons butter and 1 tablespoon oil per puffball slice
* ✳ 4 slices young giant puffball, ¾ inch (2cm) thick
* ✳ 2 tablespoons finely chopped chickweed
* ✳ 1 tablespoon Greek (strained plain) yogurt
* ✳ Crusty bread, to serve

What to do:

1 To release the cardamom seeds, put the cardamom pods in a mortar and pestle and lightly crush them (a rolling pin works well, too).

2 Peel and finely slice the carrots, and place them in a pan with the cardamom seeds and orange juice. Add enough water to cover the carrots. Bring to a boil, cover, and simmer until the carrots are soft (about 20 minutes).

3 Purée the cooked carrots and juices in a food processor.

4 Meanwhile, heat the butter and oil in a skillet (frying pan) and fry the puffball slices on both sides. Be careful not to burn the butter (the oil will help). Cook for 3–4 minutes on each side until golden. Keep the cooked puffball slices warm as you continue cooking the rest of the slices, replenishing butter and oil as required.

5 Add a final knob of butter to the skillet and wilt the chickweed. Return the carrot and cardamom purée to the pan with the chickweed, season well, and add the yogurt. Cook to heat through, and serve immediately with the puffball slices and crusty bread.

Wild Notes

Dip the puffball slices in beaten egg in a shallow dish, and then coat in toasted breadcrumbs and a sprinkling of dried sea lettuce before cooking. Sprinkle toasted wild seeds over the carrot and cardamom purée. Note that puffball slices freeze well.

This is really a soufflé-style recipe, but making the puffs in a well-oiled muffin pan makes it less frightening, and to my mind more presentable too (easier to serve). This recipe would work equally well with other species of mushroom.

Chanterelle and *Chickweed* PUFFS

Serves 8

What to forage and find:
* 1¾ cups (400ml) good chicken stock
* 2⅓ cups (150g) brushed, wiped, and thinly sliced chanterelles
* ½ stick (50g) butter
* Sea salt and freshly ground black pepper
* ¾ cup (100g) self-rising flour
* 4 eggs, lightly whisked
* 2 tablespoons finely chopped chickweed
* Oil for muffin pan
* Green salad and crusty bread, to serve

What to do:
1 Preheat the oven to 400°F (200°C/gas mark 6).

2 Put the chicken stock and chanterelles in a saucepan and bring to a boil. Add the butter and salt and pepper, and simmer gently for 3–4 minutes.

3 Remove from the heat and beat in the flour, until it leaves the pan sides clean.

4 Put the mixture into a mixing bowl, and leave to cool slightly (or the eggs will curdle). You can speed this up by standing the bowl in cold water. Then beat the lightly whisked eggs into the mixture. Stir vigorously to ensure a smooth mixture. Fold in the chopped chickweed.

5 Drizzle a little oil into 8 muffin cups and pop in the oven until the oil smokes. Remove the pan from the oven, and use a ladle to divide the mixture evenly between the cups. Bake for 15 minutes, or until the puffs are well-risen and golden.

6 Serve immediately with a green salad and crusty bread.

Folklore:

Poorer folk ate watercress because its intensely strong flavor seasoned food, and therefore avoided the need for costly imported pepper and spices.

Watercress was said to increase cows' milk production, and it was also fed to ailing cattle and horses.

About Watercress

Nasturtium officinale

"Lord, I confess too when I dine
The pulse is thine:
And all those other bits that be there
placed by thee:
The worts, the purslane, and the
mess of water-cress."
Robert Herrick, *A Thanksgiving to God, for his House*

Colloquial names:
Tongue Grass, Butter Cress, Poor Man's Pepper

Where to find:
Watercress is found in streams and ditches with moving water. Its delicate, white, four-petaled flowers appear in early spring, and for me, herald spring; watercress is one of my first spring forages. The heart-shaped leaves taste peppery, and can vary in color from vivid green to almost black.

How to forage and gather:
Do not pick watercress from stagnant water, or where sewage drains. There is much fear of liver fluke, a parasitic flatworm found on pasture land, but this is killed when watercress is cooked. It would not, however, be advisable to eat "raw" watercress, which has been picked near where cattle and sheep graze. Watercress becomes leggy after flowering, but with luck, there is another fall picking. Wear rubber boots when foraging, or, if it's warm and you can tolerate muddy feet, do it barefoot. Take scissors and a plastic bag and try not to tug at the watercress roots.

How to use:
Watercress is described as a superfood, and is now widely cultivated. It is extremely versatile and has moved well beyond being used in sandwiches It's low in fat, and rich in nutrients and vitamins, but for me, it's the peppery, slightly hot flavor that makes watercress a stand-alone.

Wash watercress well under running water, and use it raw in salads, or cooked in soups, pasta, fish, and chicken dishes. To retain its vibrant color, do not overcook it (see *Common Sorrel Sauce*, page 88). I add finely chopped watercress at the last moment to a simple supper of scrambled eggs.

About Common Sorrel

Rumex acetosa

Where to find:
In meadows, ditches, and even in garden lawns.

How to forage and gather:
Sorrel can be picked from early spring to midsummer, when the leaves toughen and it goes to seed. It may be confused with the dock leaf, which isn't poisonous but doesn't taste of lemon. Sorrel's arrow-shaped leaves are (1–4 inches/3–10cm) long, and the stems are edible, too; the ridges need to be cut from older leaves. Later in summer, sorrel has green clusters of seedy flowers, which turn pink as they age, and the leaves can become reddish, especially on the underside. French sorrel (*Rumex scuntatus*) is more common in mountainous regions and preferred by chefs due to its larger leaves.

How to use:
Before lemons were so widely available, sorrel was used in recipes. It has a sour, refreshing taste, which one of my family described as like sour apples, and, with Bog Myrtle, is on my herb "revival" list. Sorrel is rich in vitamin C, and with attention to choice of pan (use stainless steel—see *Common Sorrel Sauce*, page 88) delicious in sauces, salads, and hot and cold soups. Use it raw for maximum color.

Wood sorrel (*Oxalis aceosella*) is also versatile, albeit best used sparingly, because, like common sorrel, it has a high oxalic content. Wood sorrel has the prettiest pink and white flowers; the woods are carpeted with them in early spring.

In folklore, sorrel was used as an antiseptic and, historically, to help prevent scurvy.

Woodland & Hedgerow

Wild Watercress SAUCE

This versatile sauce is quick to make. For simplicity, omit the sorrel and replace the almonds with wild nuts or seeds.

What to do:

1 Wash and dry the watercress and put it with the almonds in a food processor. Blend briefly.

2 Add the olive oil and yogurt, and blend to mix.

3 Pour the watercress sauce into a saucepan. Add the finely shredded sorrel, and heat over low heat to warm through. Season with ground pepper. Scatter a few lady's smock flowers over the sauce. Serve with pasta, or as a sauce for salmon or poached chicken.

What to forage and find:
* 1 cup (50g) wild watercress leaves (stalks and stray roots removed)
* ⅜ cup (50g) blanched almonds
* 3 tablespoons olive oil
* 4 tablespoons Greek (strained plain) yogurt
* 1 tablespoon finely shredded sorrel
* Freshly ground black pepper

For decoration:
* 1 tablespoon watercress or lady's smock flowers, washed and dried

Common Sorrel SAUCE

This leaf is greatly underestimated: it has in many ways been replaced by lemon. It marries well with fish and chicken dishes, making a splendid green sauce. Avoid cooking sorrel in an aluminum or cast-iron saucepan, because the oxalic acid in the leaves will react and leave a metallic taste.

Makes 4–6 tablespoons, enough for 4 people

What to forage and find:
* 1 large handful (50g) young sorrel leaves (about 30 leaves)
* Scant ¼ stick (20g) butter
* ⅔ cup (150ml) heavy (double) cream
* 1 tablespoon crème fraîche
* Freshly ground black pepper

What to do:

1 Wash and dry the sorrel. Trim the stalks and remove the rib centers of any older leaves. Chiffonade the leaves (roll them tightly and finely shred).

2 Melt the butter over low heat, and wilt the sorrel for 1–2 minutes, until it loses some of its color.

3 Add the cream and crème fraîche, and stir continuously until the sauce has warmed through. Season with freshly ground pepper.

Wild Notes

use watercress instead of sorrel, or half of each, to add a peppery bite.

CHAPTER 3

FRUITS *and* Berries

About Blackberry

Rubus fruticosus

"But Flopsy, Mopsy, and Cottontail
had bread and milk and blackberries
for supper."
Beatrix Potter, *The Tale of Peter Rabbit*

Colloquial names:
Bramble, Scaldhead, Fingerberry

Where to find:
Woods, hedgerows, public land, urban areas,
gardens. It is a deciduous shrub with very
prickly, arching stems that it's easy to become
tangled in. The leaves have three to five
leaflets, and the five petaled flowers are
white or pink. The blackberry flowers in its
second year.

How to forage and gather:
Go out in late summer, with well-protected
arms, legs, and hands—wear pants/trousers,
not shorts. Rubber boots are useful footwear,
and it's a good idea to carry an antiseptic
wipe and a band-aid (plaster) in case of
scratched legs and arms. Wear old clothes,
because blackberries stain; stained mouths
are easily washed, but clothes are trickier.

Pick black or purple berries, not red.
The berry at the tip of the stem is the first
to ripen, and the sweetest. The tastiest
berries grow in direct sunlight, and will
probably be hard to access, because the
birds like "cherry-picking" blackberries,
too. There will be berries well into fall, but
these are smaller, and not as sweet as
those picked in the summer. If you pick
near public roadsides, pick as high up the
bush as you can, out of the reach of dogs
and other animals; rinse well before using
them. If you are not going to use the
blackberries immediately, refrigerate them
without washing.

How to use:
In cordials, desserts, vinegar, sauces, jellies,
and preserves. Adding crab apples or quince
will raise the pectin level of jam or jelly to
help with the set. Blackberries marry well
with apples, dissolving into a rich red pulp,
and this is a classic combination for an
autumn crumble. Blackberries are perfect for
breakfast. Pile them high on cereal, or add to
smoothies and ice cream. The blackberry also
adds vibrant color to a classic bread and
butter pudding—the delicious, dark juices
explode into the bread.

Blackberries freeze well. Lay them out on
a tray and "flash freeze" them. Pop them
into bags, and seal and label when frozen.

Folklore:
*An old wives' tale
says not to pick
blackberries after
October 10, the old
calendar date for the
Christian feast of
Michaelmas, because
the devil will come
and spit (or worse)
on the berries. Myth
suggests that the
devil fell on
blackberries on
Michaelmas Day
and cursed them.*

Blackberry and Wild Mint VINEGAR

For this colorful, store-cupboard vinegar, gather your blackberries on a fine day.

What to do:

1 Put 2¼ cups (300g) berries, a sprig of mint, and all of the vinegar into a large glass bowl. Cover, and leave to steep in a cool place for 48 hours.

2 Strain the vinegar slowly through a jelly bag, and then return it to the bowl with another 2¼ cups (300g) of freshly foraged blackberries, and another sprig of mint. Stir well, cover, and leave for 48 hours more.

3 Repeat step 2.

4 Strain through the jelly bag for a final time and measure the juice. For each 2½ cups (600ml), allow 1 lb (450g) granulated sugar.

5 Put the fruit vinegar, sugar, and fourth sprig of mint into a large saucepan, and bring to a boil. Simmer over low heat for 5 minutes, removing any scum with a slotted spoon. Leave to cool, remove the mint, and then pour into sterilized bottles, sealing them with vinegar-proof lids.

Wild Notes

Use wild raspberries and try corn mint. Pick a stem of mint and keep it in a jar of water until you need to use it.

Makes 6–8 small bottles

What to forage and find:
* 2 lb (900g) dry, ripe blackberries (3 x 2¼ cup/300g gatherings)
* 4 sprigs wild mint
* 2½ cups (600ml) cider vinegar
* Granulated sugar (see Step 4 for advice on quantity)

Blackberry and Wild Mint JUNKET

This is an adaptation of a recipe by Richard Mabey. It can be eaten as a pudding or used in a sauce, as in the recipe for *Wild Venison with Blackberry Sauce*, page 94.

Wild Notes

This junket is rich in flavor, and a small pot is sufficient. It makes a light "just set" junket, which will quickly lose its jelly-like properties when spooned. Be wary of water mint and liver fluke. Do not use mint raw if it has been gathered in streams where stock wander. Boiling kills liver fluke.

What to do:

1 Wash the blackberries and put them with the mint in a large sieve lined with cheesecloth (muslin) or a jelly bag over a bowl (or wide measuring cup), so that the juice seeps through the cheesecloth into the bowl or cup. Use the back of a spoon to push the juice through.

2 Pour the thick blackberry juice into small pots or ramekins and leave to set at room temperature. Do not refrigerate.

Makes 4 small pots

What to forage and find:
* 4 cups (500g) sweet ripe blackberries
* Sprig of mint

Fruits & Berries

This recipe is mine from my final round of *BBC Masterchef 2001*—a long time ago, but even here, I cooked using wild ingredients found where deer often graze.

WILD VENISON with *Blackberry Sauce*

Serves 4

What to forage and find:

* 18 oz (500g) boned saddle of wild red venison
* 5–6 juniper berries, crushed
* 2 sprigs of wild thyme, plus extra to garnish (optional)
* 2 tablespoons hazelnut oil
* 1 tablespoon olive oil
* 2 tablespoons + 2 teaspoons (35g) butter
* ⅓ cup (75ml) red wine
* Generous 1 cup (250ml) venison stock (made from the saddle bones)
* Small pot (scant ¼ cup/ 50ml) *Blackberry and Wild Mint Junket*, page 93, or 1 tablespoon blackberry jelly
* Salt and freshly ground black pepper, to season

What to do:

1 Preheat the oven to 350°F (180°C/gas mark 4).

2 Cut the venison into ¼-inch (5mm) slices, and put them in a shallow dish. Scatter with the juniper berries and thyme, and pour over the hazelnut oil. Cover and refrigerate for 1½ hours.

3 Heat the olive oil and 2 tablespoons (25g) butter in a skillet (frying pan), sear the venison quickly on each side, and reserve the pan juices.

4 Place the venison in an ovenproof dish, cover with foil, and cook for 5–8 minutes —the venison should remain pink.

5 Add the wine to the reserved pan juices and reduce by half, then add the stock, and reduce again. Add the blackberry junket. Finally, add the remaining 2 teaspoons (10g) of butter. Season, and serve the venison with the blackberry sauce poured over it.

Wild Notes

Use rowan jelly instead of blackberry junket.

Fruits & Berries

94

Red Cabbage and VENISON with *Pontack Sauce*

Slow-cooked red cabbage mingled with wild fruits goes perfectly with venison. Replace the sausages with pan-fried venison steaks for a dinner party.

Serves 4

What to do:

1 On the stovetop (hob), heat the oil in an ovenproof casserole dish, and lightly brown the sausages. Add the onion, cabbage, and sugar, and cook briefly for 1–2 minutes. Add the spices and vegetable stock, and bring to a boil.

2 Add the pontack sauce, season, and cover with a lid. Either cook on the stovetop on very low heat until the cabbage is soft, and has absorbed most of the stock (about 1 hour), or braise the cabbage in a low oven—300°F (150°C/ gas mark 2)—until soft, about 2 hours.

3 Halfway through the cooking time, add the blackberries.

Wild Notes

The easiest way to pick elderberries is to cut the umbel with scissors. Place the berries into a bowl and fill with water so that the green berries and twig debris floats to the top. Use a small sieve to skim any chaff from the surface. Drain the berries and they are ready to use in the kitchen.

What to forage and find:
* 1 tablespoon olive oil
* 8 venison sausages
* 1 small red onion, finely chopped
* ½ red cabbage (1 lb/450g), heart removed and finely sliced
* 1 tablespoon brown sugar
* 8 juniper berries
* 2 allspice berries
* 1 star anise
* 1½ cups (350ml) vegetable stock
* 2 tablespoons *Pontack Sauce*, see below
* Salt and freshly ground black pepper, to season
* ⅜ cup (50g) blackberries

Pontack Sauce

This rich sauce recipe is an adaptation of *Elderberry Ketchup* from Mrs M. Grieve's *A Modern Herbal*, introduced by Mrs C.F. Lyell. A few splashes make a wonderful addition to game casseroles, but it is equally good with cold meats, cheese, and potato cakes, or *Red Berries and Meadowsweet Pudding*, page 117.

Makes 3 small bottles

What to do:

1 Put the elderberries in a jar or unglazed ovenproof casserole dish with the vinegar, cover, and cook overnight in the simmering oven of a range oven at 250°F (120°C/gas mark ½), or in a crockpot (slow cooker) on low.

2 Next day, strain the juices through cheesecloth (muslin) or a jelly bag into a saucepan. Squeeze the berries to remove as much juice as possible. Add the rest of

the ingredients, apart from the sugar. Bring to a boil and simmer over a very low heat for 45 minutes. Add the sugar, cook over low heat to dissolve, then boil rapidly for 5 minutes until rich and syrupy.

3 Strain into a pitcher (jug). When cold, pour the pontack into small, sterilized, screwtop bottles. I use 3½ fl oz (100ml) bottles. Store in a cool, dark place to allow the flavors to mature.

What to forage and find:
* 2¼ lb (500g) elderberries, destalked and washed
* Scant 1½ cups (350ml) cider vinegar
* Large red onion, peeled and thinly sliced
* 3 allspice berries
* 1 teaspoon black peppercorns
* 1 star anise
* 1¼ inches (3cm) fresh ginger, bashed
* 5–6 cloves
* 2½ tablespoons brown sugar

Fruits & Berries

Foraging can be arduous, but sometimes you come across a heavily laden crab apple tree, or blackberry bush, and this is the time to think about making fruit leathers. If the fruit is sweet, there isn't any need to add sugar or honey, but if you've foraged crab apples, you'll need some. This straightforward snack is simply condensed (puréed) fruit dried until it becomes leather-like—easy peasy. I make this wicked blackberry leathers recipe for Halloween, but you can, if you are fortunate enough to forage lots of berries, make it with raspberries or strawberries. Raspberries, wild strawberries, and blackberries can be dried individually in a food dehydrator, and added to muesli, or eaten as a snack.

Blackberry and *Wild Thyme* LEATHERS

What to do:

1 Put the blackberries and lemon juice in a food processor and blend well. Add sugar to taste.

2 Push the blackberry purée through a plastic sieve and drain into a pitcher (jug). You should have about 1¾ cups (400ml) of purée.

3 If using a food dehydrator, pour the purée as thinly as possible over 3–4 racks lined with parchment paper. Drying time will be dependent on the thickness of the purée and the type of machine used. I move the layers around during drying time, because the top will dry quicker than the bottom. I find it easier to allow the leather to cool before removing the paper.

4 Cut the leathers into strips, and roll into coils, or roll into one thick length and cut into more substantial leathers. Store in an airtight container.

To oven dry:

If you don't have a food dehydrator, divide the purée between two oven trays, lined with parchment paper or oiled foil. You need a smooth, thin layer no thicker than a piece of paper. It is important to spread the purée evenly, or thinner edges will cook/dry too quickly. Bake at the lowest temperature the oven will register for 12–24 hours, until the purée is dry and peels away from the paper or foil with ease. Watch the color as the purée begins to dry out; it may be necessary to prop open the oven door to continue drying very slowly.

Makes 4 thin layers, about 35–40 strips

What to forage and find:
* 4½ cups (600g) washed blackberries
* Juice of 1 small lemon
* 3–4 teaspoons wild thyme sugar, to taste (see page 15)

Fruits & Berries

98

Wild Notes

Children will enjoy eating fruit leathers, and they are fun to make, too. Children can stamp out tiny stars, or even butterflies, using miniature aspic jelly cutters available from craft shops. This recipe can be adapted for any wild fruit. Leathers can also be made with autumn berries such as rose hips and hawthorn berries, and stewed quince or apple. Cook the fruit or berries in a saucepan with lemon juice and minimal water until they are soft, then push the mixture through a sieve. Add sugar to taste to the warm, sieved purée. The end result will definitely boost your vitamin C level.

Here is a lazy cook's tip for lining a food dehydrator—use a flattened parchment cake-pan (tin) liner.

About Bilberries

Vaccinium myrtillus

"In Gweithdy Bach we'll rest awhile,
We'll dress our wounds and learn
to smile
With easier lips; we'll stretch our legs,
And live on bilberry tart and eggs."
Robert Graves, *A Letter to Siegfried Sassoon
from Mametz Wood*

Colloquial names:

Blaeberry (Scotland), Bog Bilberry, Bog
Blueberry, Bog Whortleberry, Bog
Huckleberry, Ground Hurts, Northern
Bilberry, Windberry, Wimberry,
Whortleberry Fraughan (Ireland),
Black-Hearts

Where to find:

Bilberries lurk among heathers on moor
or heathland, or under trees in mature
woodland. Although tricky to spy initially,
once you get your eye in, you will be richly
rewarded—the taste of the tiny blue berry
(resembling a small blueberry) is delicious. In
mid-spring, singular, greenish-pink flowers
precede the highly prized berries of summer.
The oval-shaped leaves are bright green.

How to forage and gather:

In contrast to blackberries, which are
common or garden to most foragers, one of
the most difficult tiny, black berries to harvest
is the bilberry. There is often only one berry
on each low-lying stem of the deciduous
bush. Occasionally, they are paired, but,
nevertheless, harvesting them is hard work
and is best done on hands and knees.

How to use:

Bilberries are scrumptious raw, but even
sweeter (in my opinion) when cooked. They
can be used in recipes that call for blueberries
but I particularly like them with venison,
an idea inspired by Maxine Clark, a Scots

venison cook. They are also useful dried; a
food dehydrator makes this an easy task, but
I then find myself counting the number of
dried bilberries that I'm prepared to add to
homemade muesli, because their gathering
really is a true labor of love.

My daughter, Lili, and I picked for well
over an hour on a heather moor (with the
landowner's foraging permission) but still
picked less than 4 oz (110g)—just enough
for a batch of bilberry muffins (see *Sea Kelp
Muffins*, page 172, which can be adapted
for bilberries).

Folklore:

On August 1st, the
Gaelic festival of
Lughnasadh would
pass judgment on the
harvest of the bilberry
crop, as a gauge of the
potential of later crops.
In Ireland, bilberries are
traditionally collected
on Fraughan Sunday,
which is the last
Sunday in July.

Bilberries were used
as a dye in the First
World War—small
wonder that my
children, when
younger, often
returned home from
hill walks with
bilberry-stained faces.
Richard Mabey writes
of Somerset bilberry
pickers wearing rain
(wellington) boots to
protect themselves from
adders, but goes on
to suggest that the idea
of snakes may have
served as a suitable
deterrent to "outsider"
foragers. I smiled as I
read this, and repeat
my foraging message:
gather for your own
supper table, don't pick
more than one-sixth of
any leaf, fruit, fungi,
or blossom, and avoid
picking roots unless
the plant is invasive.

Pan-fried Pigeon and *Bilberry* salad

Fall is woodpigeon season. With luck, bilberries will still be around but, if not, this fast-cooking recipe also works well with blackberries and elderberries.

Serves 4

What to forage and find:
* 7 oz (200g) mixed wild salad leaves, about 8 handfuls (see *Wild Notes* below)
* 4 pigeon breasts
* Sea salt and freshly ground black pepper
* Knob of butter
* 3 tablespoons mild vegetable oil
* 2 tablespoons *Blackberry and Wild Water Mint Vinegar*, page 93
* 2 tablespoons olive oil
* 4 tablespoons bilberries

What to do:

1 Preheat the oven to 400°F (200°C/ gas mark 6).

2 Wash the salad leaves and dry them really well. This ensures that the vinaigrette will stick to the leaves.

3 Season the pigeon with salt and pepper (or a pinch of dried sea lettuce).

4 Heat an ovenproof skillet (frying pan) until hot, and then add the butter and 1 tablespoon of the oil. Cook the pigeon breasts, starting skin side down, for a minute on each side, and then transfer the pan to the oven for 3 minutes. Remove the pan from the oven, and put the pigeon onto a serving plate. Cover with foil, and leave to rest for another 3 minutes. Cut each breast thinly into 4 slices and re-cover with the foil.

5 Return the skillet to the stovetop (hob) and deglaze the pigeon juices with the blackberry vinegar. Whisk in the remaining oils, cook briefly, and remove from the heat. Season to taste.

6 Divide the wild salad leaves between four plates and arrange the pigeon slices on the beds of salad. Scatter the bilberries over the pigeon, and drizzle a little warm blackberry vinaigrette over the salad leaves on each plate. Serve immediately.

Wild Notes

I rarely find enough bilberries to make vinegar, but this recipe would be delicious with bilberry vinegar (adapt the blackberry vinegar recipe, page 93). For added spice, add 2–3 finely chopped pickled ramps (wild garlic) when you deglaze the pan. In fall, make this salad with a warm Pontack Sauce, page 99, substituting the bilberries for blackberries or elderberries.

The problem I find with wild leaves and salads is that they are best eaten in late spring and early summer, and as there are bilberries in this recipe, many will be past their best. "Young" is a key word when gathering wild leaves. In fall, sprinkle salads with toasted, edible flower seeds. Young salad and wild garlic leaves can be used as wraps (dolmas).

Here is a far from comprehensive list of edible wild leaves that I have used in salads: one star means eat in spring/early summer. Two stars means use sparingly.

Blackberry*
Chickweed
Dandelion leaves*
Young dock leaves
Hawthorn*
Hazelnut*
Lady's smock*
Lovage**
Salad burnet*
Sea purslane
Sorrel**
Watercress
Wild garlic **
Growing tips of willow herb *

Fruits & Berries

101

Served in a watermelon, this refreshing drink, bouncing with tiny wild fruits, will steal the show. Add wild strawberries if they are available.

Watermelon, *Bilberry,* and Wild Mint Cooler

Serves 6

What to forage and find:
* Watermelon
* 3 wild mint leaves, finely shredded
* 3½ cups (800ml) blueberry juice
* ⅜ cup (50g) bilberries
* Borage ice cubes (see *Borage, How to use,* page 149)
* Angelica, sweet cicely, or lovage straws (optional)

What to do:

1 Take a sharp knife and slice off the top of the watermelon, about 1½–2 inches (4–5cm) from the top. Use a melon-ball scoop to gouge melon balls from the top (lid).

2 Pour any watermelon juice through a sieve with the mint leaves. Set the juice aside.

3 Put the melon balls into a bowl and set aside for a fruit salad. Continue to remove the flesh from the melon using the melon-ball scoop, to leave an empty shell (to fill with juice). When the melon balls begin to look "scruffy", scoop out the remaining melon with a spoon and put it in the sieve.

4 Remove any wayward seeds, but leave the mint leaves, and blitz flesh, mint leaves, and juice in a food processor. Sieve again and add to the juice from step 2.

5 Pour the drained and sieved minted watermelon juice into the empty watermelon shell, and top up with blueberry juice (approximately 3½ cups/ 800ml), depending on the size of the melon and amount of juice extracted.

6 Add the bilberries and borage ice cubes and use angelica, sweet cicely, or lovage straws to drink straight from the watermelon. Or pour the juice into a pitcher (jug) and serve in individual glasses with the wild straws, bilberries, and borage ice cubes.

Wild Notes

You may prefer to gouge out chunks of melon and then stamp small stars or other shapes from the melon—children will enjoy doing this.

Fruits & Berries

Served hot from the oven with ice cream or custard, this cake can be used as pudding, but it is equally delicious cold at teatime.

Bilberry and HAZELNUT CRUMBLE Cake

Serves 8

What to forage and find:
For the cake:
* 7 oz (200g) soft margarine
* 1 cup (200g) superfine (caster) sugar
* 3 eggs
* 1½ cups (200g) sifted self-rising flour
* Milk (if required)
* 1¼ cups (150g) bilberries, washed and dried

For the crumble:
* ½ stick (50g) salted butter
* Heaping ½ cup (75g) all-purpose (plain) flour
* ¼ cup (25g) hazelnuts, ground
* 2 tablespoons (25g) soft brown sugar

What to do:
1 Preheat the oven to 375°F (190°C/gas mark 5).

2 Line an 8-inch (20cm) cake pan (tin) with parchment paper.

3 To prepare the crumble, put the butter and flour into a bowl, and rub together until it resembles breadcrumbs. Add the hazelnuts and sugar, and set aside.

4 To make the cake, cream the margarine and sugar in a bowl until soft and fluffy.

5 Lightly beat the eggs, and slowly beat them into the margarine and sugar mixture, adding a spoonful of sifted flour with the last third of the beaten eggs.

6 Fold in the remaining flour, adding a tablespoon of milk if necessary (the mixture should fall slowly from the spoon).

7 Turn the cake mixture into the prepared pan, and smooth with a knife.

8 Scatter the bilberries over the mixture, and sprinkle the crumble over the top.

9 Bake for 45–50 minutes, or until the cake feels firm, and a toothpick inserted into the center comes out clean.

Wild Notes

If you are fortunate enough to forage wild cranberries, cook them with sugar and a little orange juice, and use in place of bilberries.

I get the best results from frozen bilberries —the color explodes as they defrost.

Bilberry and Lime Posset

In medieval times, a posset was a curdled wine but it is now associated with a syllabub pudding. This simple recipe could be adapted to elder or other wild blossom by infusing the blossoms in the cream at step 1. Elderflowers were traditionally added to a summer baby's christening posset.

Makes 6–7 small pots

What to forage and find:
* Generous 2 cups (500ml) heavy (double) cream
* ¾ cup (150g) superfine (caster) sugar
* Zest of 1 lime, plus extra to garnish
* Juice of 2 limes
* ¾ cup (100g) bilberries, washed and dried

What to do:

1 Put the cream, sugar, and lime zest in a heavy-based saucepan, and cook over low heat until the sugar dissolves (3–4 minutes). Remove from the heat.

2 Whisk the lime juice into the cream (it will thicken).

3 Divide half of the bilberries between the pots and pour in half of the lime cream. Scatter most of the remaining bilberries on top of the cream (reserving 6–7 for decoration) and then divide the rest of the lime cream between the pots. Decorate each pot with a bilberry and lime zest.

4 Leave to cool, and then refrigerate.

Wild Notes

Purée wild fruits and layer with the posset in a glass. Sea buckthorn berries work well, but you can use any soft wild fruit, or edible (and not protected) wildflowers in a posset. Try sweet violets: substitute the lime for the more traditional lemon, and swirl in some color with a splash of Sweet Violet Syrup, page 38. A dash of Honeysuckle Syrup, page 26, will sweeten a blackberry posset, or a drizzle of Pontack Sauce, page 97, will spice it up.

About Quince

Cydonia vulgaris

"They dined on mince,
and slices of quince,
which they ate with a runcible spoon."
Edward Lear, *The Owl and The Pussycat*

Where to find:

The quince tree will thrive almost anywhere,
suggests Mrs Grieve in *A Modern Herbal*.
I certainly know of a "survivor" close to
my mother's house; workmen are forever
investigating nearby, and still the quince
tree bears fruit. In spring, the pink or white
blossom on the quince tree is stunning, and
has the most delicate scent. The flower
blooms after the tree has leafed. The quince
itself varies in size and shape, although it
could be described as a rounded, pear-
shaped fruit. The fruit, and underside of its
leaves, are covered in fine down when ripe.

How to forage and gather:

Pick quince as you would an apple in early
fall, but, unlike the apple, it can still be found
in late fall.

How to use:

Quince is not palatable raw, because it is very
hard, but then the magic happens; it softens
on cooking, the fruit turns orangey-red, and
the taste is exquisite. However, you
can't hurry the cooking process; long, slow
poaching is my preferred way. The seeds of
the quince are very high in pectin, so the fruit
marries well in jellies to fruits with lower
pectin levels. Quince is hard to cut, and tricky
to peel, so I don't bother doing either.

You might find a recipe for Quince
Butter, or you may prefer to make *Quince
Paste (Membrillo)*, page 110 (usually eaten
in Portugal and Spain with cream cheese
and crackers).

You can coat ham and salmon with
quince syrup (reduce *Quince Cordial*,

page 110, to a syrup) and quinces can be
used to make chutney, jelly, and ice cream.
Quince is delicious in casseroles with
pheasant or chicken. You can also add a
poached or roasted quince to brighten up
a dull apple crumble or sauce. Chunks of
scrubbed quince (to remove the down) can
be packed into wide-necked jars, and then
covered with gin or grappa, sealed,
and stored for a few months to make a
delicious digestif.

Folklore:

The quince was
dedicated to Venus
and was thus
regarded as the
symbol of love. In
ancient Athens,
the bride and groom
ate a quince together
on entering the
bridal chamber to
ensure a sweet
and affectionate
relationship—I
presume the quince
was cooked.

Quince and Wild Thyme SORBET

This recipe also works well with crushed pink peppercorns instead of wild thyme.

Serves 4
Makes approximately
2½ cups (600ml)

What to forage and find:
* 6 quinces (about
  2 lb/900g)
* ¾ cup (150g) superfine
  (caster) sugar
* ½ cup (100g) wild
  thyme sugar (see *Wild
  Notes*, right)
* 3¾ cups (750ml) water
* Juice of ½ lemon
* 1 egg white, lightly
  whisked

What to do:
1 Put the quinces and superfine sugar in a saucepan with water to cover (2½ cups/600ml). Bring the pan to a boil, cover, and simmer until the quinces are very soft (about 3 hours). When the fruit is cool enough to handle, push it through a sieve.

2 Put the wild thyme sugar and the rest of the water in a saucepan, and heat gently, stirring frequently to dissolve the sugar. Bring to a boil, and boil for 5 minutes until you have a light syrup. Remove from the heat, and leave to cool completely.

3 Mix the cold, pink quince purée and lemon juice with the cooled syrup. Put the mixture in an ice-cream machine and churn until frozen.

4 When the sorbet is just beginning to set, add the lightly whisked egg white and continue to freeze.

> *Wild Notes*
>
> If you don't have wild thyme sugar, add two sprigs of wild thyme to the water and sugar when you make the sorbet. Remove after infusing the sugar syrup.

5 If you don't have an ice-cream machine: put the sorbet into a freezer-safe container and freeze until slushy. Return the mixture to the bowl, beat well (or whiz in a food processor), and return to the freezer. Repeat this process until you can't see any icy crystals, then freeze until frozen.

Edible berries:

A berry to look out for is sea buckthorn or sea berry (*Hippophae rhamnoides*). The wonderful golden-orange berries are found in coastal areas between late summer and mid-fall (it tolerates salt). The branches are thorny, and the best way to remove the berries is to give it a good shake with glove-clad hands. Once harvested, the berries make tart, but delicious, jellies and when puréed and sieved, an interesting orange sorbet. Sea buckthorn appears to be on the rise as a new superfood for the forager: the good news in health terms is that a small amount will go a long way. Until recently, the berries have been left to the birds, but the Danes have long used it to make schnapps. It can be used to make cordials, and I have added it to apple dishes, for its color. The smell of sea buckthorn is unpleasant, but its tart, high-in-pectin berries are delicious, and worth thorny and scent discomforts during harvesting.

> *Wild Notes*
>
> These are my favorite edible berries (the list is far from comprehensive).
>
> Elder
> Hawthorn
> Rosehip
> Rowan
> Sea buckthorn

Quince Cordial

This cordial is an adaptation of a recipe by Skye Gyngell.

Makes about 1¼ quarts
(1.2 liters)

What to forage and find:
* 12 quinces
* 1¾ cups (350g)
  superfine (caster) sugar,
  to taste
* About 1 quart (1 liter)
  water

What to do:

1 Preheat the oven to 325°F (160°C/gas mark 3).

2 Put the quinces and water to cover in a large roasting pan (tin) and cover with foil.

3 Bake for 3–4 hours until the quinces are completely soft and the juices are ruby-red.

4 Strain the liquid into a pitcher (jug) and reserve the poached quinces to eat with other fruits in a compote.

Quince Paste

Delicious with cold meats and cheese, this is also a useful sweetener for stewed fruits.

Makes 4 small jars

What to forage and find:
* 2¼ lb (1kg) quinces (no
  need to peel and core)
* 2 generous cups
  (500ml) water
* 2 limes
* Granulated sugar
  (see Step 2 for advice
  on quantity)
* Lemons

What to do:

1 Wash and roughly chop the quinces and put them in a preserving (heavy-based) pan with the water and juice of two limes. Bring to a boil, then simmer until the quinces are very soft (1½ hours or longer; you can do this in a low oven or pressure cooker if preferred).

2 Remove the pan from the heat, cool slightly, then blend the pulp in a food processor before pushing it through a sieve into a bowl. This takes time. Weigh the quince pulp and return it to the pan, adding an equal amount of sugar to pulp and the juice of a small lemon to each 1 lb (450g) of sugar.

3 Return the heavy-based pan to low heat, stirring continuously until the sugar has dissolved.

4 Continue to cook until the quince paste is very thick, stirring frequently. This will take at least an hour—slowly the color will change from caramel to dark red. Be careful not to let the quince catch the bottom of the pan and burn. The quince paste is ready when it stays on the spoon, i.e. it doesn't slide off the wooden spoon back into the pan. Pour into warm, sterilized jars and seal.

Wild Notes

Replace some of the sugar with a few tablespoons of Honeysuckle Syrup, page 26.

About Wild Plums

Prunus insititia (bullaces)
Prunus spinosa (blackthorn or sloe)
Prunus domestica (damson)

"To market, to market
To buy a plum bun.
Home again, home again,
Market is done."
John Florio, *Worlde of Wordes* (1611)

Colloquial names:
Bully Tree, Bullison, Bullies, Winter Crack, Bullace, Damson, Damson Plum, Scad, Mirabelle

Where to find:
You may be lucky enough to find plum trees growing in the wild; I certainly know of one or two left over from abandoned orchards. Forage smugly, but abstemiously, for your own pies and jam, and count yourself lucky. The damson is said to take its name from "Plum of Damascus," having been cultivated there. It is much smaller than the garden plum, and dark bluish-purple in color. In my foraging experience, the trees are quite hard to find. The blossom on the sloe and bullace bush is pretty, as is that of the damson tree. Mid- to late-spring blossom will mark the spot of a fall bounty. The small, dark blue sloe is the fruit of the blackthorn, which is a bush not a tree, and do take note of the word thorn.

Bullaces are often muddled with sloes. They, too, grow on bushes, but are larger and sweeter; a quick taste will differentiate between the two. The sloe leaf is long, while the bullace leaf is round, and the bullace bushes have few, if any thorns. Bullaces and sloes are found in hedgerows, old gardens, and abandoned wasteland. I once found a particularly large patch on chalkland.

How to forage and gather:
Although bullaces aren't as sour as sloes, they, too, are best harvested after the first frost, when they are bletted (softened). The frost softens the flesh, and decreases the acidity of the berry. Sometimes a tardy harvest means that the berries have begun to wither, or an earlier hunter has already gathered, so clever foragers home-freeze the berries before using them. I always carry antiseptic wipes when foraging the sloe berry. The bush has a thorny reputation, and has been known to puncture the bicycle tire (tyre) of a careless forager.

How to use:
Bullaces, damsons, and sloes can be soaked in gin, vodka, or whisky. After drinking sloe gin, keep the bitter sloes and dip them in melted chocolate. Damsons make delicious spiced jelly and curds, and all three add color to fall crumbles, cobblers, hedgerow jams, and chutneys. Bullaces are particularly good in a sauce with breast of woodpigeon, and fillet of pork works well with damsons.

Folklore:
In Westmoreland, Cumbria, a Sunday in April was called "Damson Sunday" because tourists could behold the beauty of the white blossom. The plums were also used to dye cloth in the textile industry.

Mini *Damson* TARTES TATINS

I wonder what little Jack Horner would have thought of these "just a mouthful", upside-down tarts. If you have time, make your own rough puff pastry, which will make these wee tarts even more mouth-watering.

What to do:

1 Preheat the oven to 400°F (200°C/gas mark 6).

2 Cut the damsons in half, and remove the pits (stones). In a muffin pan (tin), put 6 damson halves, skin side down, in each muffin cup, filling 10 cups.

3 Meanwhile, heat the sugar and butter in a saucepan over low heat until melted. Stir well, and divide the mixture between the 10 cups.

4 Lightly dust a working surface with flour, and roll out the pastry. Use a cutter to stamp out 10 x 3-inch (7.5cm) circles. Put a pastry circle on top of each filled muffin cup.

5 Bake for 10–12 minutes, until the pastry is risen and golden.

6 Take the tarts out of the oven, cool for a minute, and then run a knife around the pastry to loosen it. If you are brave: put a tray over the muffin pan, turn the muffin pan upside down, and fingers crossed, the mini damson tartes tatins will turn out on to the tray. Alternatively, spoon the pastry (base) onto a serving dish, and spoon the damsons back on top. Either way, it's yummy.

7 These are delicious cold or warm, with yogurt or ice cream.

Makes 10 small tarts

What to forage and find:

* About 2 cups (200g) wild damson plums, washed (approximately 30 plums)
* ⅓ cup (75g) soft light brown (light muscovado) sugar
* 2 generous tablespoons (35g) butter
* All-purpose (plain) flour, for dusting
* 10½ x 8-inch (27 x 20cm) sheet puff pastry
* Yogurt or ice cream, to serve

Wild Notes

In season, replace the damsons or plums with wild cherries.

About Crab Apple

Malus sylvestris

"A hundred and three come January,
I've one tooth left in my head, said he
Timothy under the crab-apple tree."
Wilfrid Wilson Gibson

Where to find:
Standing as grand as any parkland tree,
the crab apple is a small, handsome,
deciduous tree, found in woodlands and
hedgerows. The blossoms are beautiful,
with the five-petaled flowers appearing
in clusters.

How to forage and gather:
Like other apple trees, the crab apple fruits
in late summer through to early fall. The
hard fruits vary in color from light green,
to yellow, to a rosy pink. Some people say
they are better collected after the first frost,
which softens them. The fairy-sized fruit
is bitter.

How to use:
Crab apples can be pickled with sweet
spices, made into chutney, or cooked
with sweet apples to add tartness. I have a
"help cook" fondness for them: the high
pectin content makes them useful in jelly
making. See *Crab Apple and Wild
Honeysuckle Jelly*, opposite.

In France they use crab apples to make
verjuice, an acidulant. If you have a juicer,
I suspect this would make that particular
process easier. You can also use crab apples
to make fruit pastes. See *Quince Paste*,
page 110.

Honeysuckle gives a delicate flavor to crab apple jelly, which can be rather bland. I've made a stand-alone honeysuckle jelly, too, and was intrigued that it set without pectin.

Crab Apple and Wild Honeysuckle Jelly

What to do:

1 Put the honeysuckle flowers in a preserving pan, and cover them with boiling water. Leave to steep overnight.

2 Wash the crab apples, removing any stalks and leaves, and add them to the honeysuckle and water. The water should just cover the crab apples—add more water if necessary. Bring the pan to a boil, and simmer until the crab apples are very soft (about 45 minutes).

3 Strain the fruit through a jelly bag. (I leave it overnight). Don't be tempted to squeeze the jelly bag or the resulting jelly will be cloudy.

4 Measure the juice, and pour it into the preserving pan with the lemon juice. Bring to a boil, then add the sugar. For each 2½ cups (600ml) of juice, add 1 lb (450g) of granulated sugar. Dissolve the sugar over low heat, then bring the pan to a rolling boil for about 10 minutes until setting point is reached.*

5 Use a slotted spoon to remove the scum, and pour the jelly into warm, sterilized jars. Cover and label.

* To test for setting point, drop a little jelly onto a cold saucer (from the fridge), wait for 30 seconds, and if the jelly crinkles when pushed with a finger, the jelly will set.

Makes 4 small jars

What to forage and find:
* 10 wild honeysuckle blossoms, washed
* 3¼ lb (1.5kg) crab apples
* Juice of 1 small lemon
* Granulated sugar (see Step 4 for advice on quantity)

Wild Notes
In spring, the crab apple's blousy pink and white flowers attract bees, butterflies, and lots of other insect visitors. Birds also feed on it—it is such a useful tree.

About Wild Strawberries

Fragaria vesca

"A pot of strawberries gathered in the wood to mingle with your cream."
Ben Jonson (1603)

Colloquial names:
Woodland Strawberries, Fraise des Bois, Alpine Strawberries

Where to find:
In woodland, grassy banks, old garden patios, railway embankments, country lanes, and scrubland. The tiny, scarlet, fragrant berries are covered with small seeds, and hide under sprawling runners. The trefoil leaves roughen on maturity and the white flowers, borne irregularly, have five exquisite petals. There are woods behind our Angus garden, and the invasive strawberry plant has gradually wound its way to the back door, via a jagged and irregular path of flagstones—making it so easy to pick a berry and drop it into a summer glass of Pimms.

How to forage and gather:
Woodland strawberries fruit in early summer, but alpine plants produce a few ripe berries on each plant all summer, on an almost daily basis. Don't pick overripe berries; seek out those that are uniformly red with darkened seeds. The leaves can also be collected (sparingly, a couple from each plant) for tisanes and salads.

The little berries are delicious, but, as there are rarely more than a couple on each plant, gathering the pot described by Ben Jonson would have been a labor of love. Due to their fragility, the strawberries need to be placed carefully in a small, shallow basket to avoid crushing and spoiling.

How to use:
The small berries can be dried and used in granola but I prefer them fresh from the wild, sprinkled on cereal, or, on a cold summer morning in Scotland, on oatmeal (porridge). Serve them in drinks, with pancakes, such as *Elderflower Scented Pancakes*, page 17, in possets (see *Bilberry and Lime Posset*, page 106) or with ice cream.

Folklore:
Cut berries are said to ease sunburn, and were used to clean teeth. Modern medicine calls the strawberry birthmark a "vascular nevus," but it was once thought to be the mark of royalty, or possibly due to the pregnant woman's craving for strawberries. The wild strawberry was mentioned in the writings of Pliny, and garlands of it appear in medieval art—in art it had no season.

Red Berries and Meadowsweet Pudding

This is a variation on a summer favorite, using brioche and red berries infused with meadowsweet.

Serves 6–8

What to forage and find:

* 18 oz (500g) fresh raspberries
* 2 cups (200g) fresh red currants
* Large sprig meadowsweet (including leaves)
* 2 tablespoons water (or diluted meadowsweet syrup)
* 6 tablespoons–½ cup (75–100g sugar), to taste
* 2 cups (200g) fresh strawberries
* 1 loaf stale brioche (or 8 individual brioches)
* Cream or Greek (strained plain) yogurt, to serve

What to do:

1 Gently simmer the raspberries, red currants, meadowsweet, water, and sugar over low heat until the berry juices begin to run (3–4 minutes). Then add the strawberries, and cook for another 2 minutes, until the strawberries are just soft. Remove from the heat, and leave until cold to allow the meadowsweet to infuse.

2 Line a medium pudding mold with plastic wrap (clingfilm), then line the base and sides with ⅜-inch (1cm) slices of brioche, making sure not to leave any gaps.

3 Remove the meadowsweet from the berries, and fill the brioche-lined bowl with the fruit and juice.

4 Cover the top of the bowl with slices of brioche, again filling any gaps. Put a small plate over the top of the bowl, and weigh it down. Leave in a cool place for 24 hours to allow the fruit juices to soak into the brioche.

5 Invert the pudding onto a serving dish, and remove the plastic wrap (clingfilm). Serve sliced, with cream or Greek (strained plain) yogurt.

Wild Notes

Use elderflower instead of meadowsweet, and as the season progresses, replace the berries with fall fruits: blackberries, and elderberries flavored with Pontack Sauce, page 97.

Fruits & Berries

117

About Gooseberries

Ribes uva-crispa

" 'Country life has its conveniences,' he would sometimes say. 'You sit on the verandah and you drink tea, while your ducks swim on the pond, there is a delicious smell everywhere… and the gooseberries are growing.' "
Anton Chekhov, "Gooseberries", *The Wife and Other Stories*

Colloquial names:

Grosberry, Fayberry, Feaberry Feverberry, Worcesterberry, Goosegog, Grosset

Where to find:

These are not the most common fruits to find growing wild, and are more widespread in the UK than the US. Bushes grow in woods, on the edge of cultivated patches, wasteland, banks of canals, and meadow hedges on moist ground. My favorite patch to forage is on the banks of a small burn (stream).

The largest member of the red currant and black currant family (*Grossulariaceae*), the gooseberry bush is distinctive for its thorns, maple-shaped lobed leaves, which are slightly hairy underneath, and single berries. The berries vary in color from green to the sweetest red. The berries have bristly, fine hairs, but these disappear on cooking.

How to forage and gather:

Gooseberries are found from late spring to late summer. Wear stout gloves to protect your hands from the thorns, and as with all wild berries, be prepared for the fruits to be much smaller than those of cultivated gooseberry varieties. Picking wild berrries takes time.

How to use:

The bittersweet taste of gooseberries is one that, in my opinion, deserves a minimum of sugar, but many will find the early green berries too tart without ample sweetener. I cook mine with the leaves of sweet cicely or, later in summer, meadowsweet and sugar to taste. Gooseberries are seldom eaten raw. As a rule of thumb, the smaller the fruit, the higher the acidity. "Top and tailing" (the removal of the stalks) is tedious but necessary for crumbles and tarts; use a sharp knife or scissors. This can be avoided if the recipe involves sieving or straining the cooked berries. Gooseberries can be used in: chutneys, fools, syrups, desserts, ice cream, and sauces for rich meats and fish. The acidity of the gooseberry cuts through the oiliness of mackerel; this is a classic recipe combination. The strained tart juice is a useful substitute for lemon in salad dressings. Gooseberries are particularly good in jams and jellies because of their high pectin content, and they freeze well.

Gooseberries are high in vitamin C and contain plenty of fiber as well as vitamins A and D, and minerals.

Folklore:

What's in the name? It is often said that the word gooseberry came from the berries being used in a sauce that accompanied goose. A green sauce was served with young gosling in the summer, but it is doubtful that gooseberries would have been eaten with goose at Christmas, because they weren't in season. In *The Englishman's Flora*, Geoffrey Grigson suggests that gooseberry comes from the French word for red currant: *groseille*, which is in the same family.

The fairies were said to have sheltered from danger in the prickly gooseberry bushes, hence the name, Fayberries.

Wild Gooseberry and Elderflower Ice Cream

A dreamy, midsummer, wild ice cream, which will leave many playing the food guessing game. Eat this ice cream immediately, do not refreeze it.

What to do:

1 Put the cordial and sugar in a clean saucepan over low heat, and stir until the sugar dissolves. Boil rapidly for 3–4 minutes, and remove from the heat. Add the elderflower heads, and leave to infuse for 2–3 hours. Strain the elderflower syrup through a sieve into another pan.

2 Add the gooseberries to the syrup, cover, and simmer until the gooseberries are soft. Taste, adding sugar if required. Blend the gooseberries in a food processor, then sieve the seeds through a nylon sieve, pushing the smooth purée into a bowl with the back of a spoon. Set aside until cool.

3 Stir the cream into the cooled gooseberry and elderflower purée and churn in an ice-cream machine until frozen.

4 If you don't have an ice-cream machine: put the gooseberry ice-cream into a freezer-safe container, and freeze until slushy. Return the mixture to the bowl, beat well (or whiz in a food processor), and return to the freezer. Repeat this process until you can't see any ice crystals, and then freeze solid. Allow the ice cream to soften in a refrigerator before serving.

Serves 4

What to forage and find:
* 1 cup (250ml) diluted *Elderflower Cordial*, page 20
* ½ cup (100g) superfine (caster) sugar
* 3 elderflower heads (well shaken, not washed)
* 4 cups (1 lb/450g) gooseberries, washed (but no need to top and tail)
* Additional superfine sugar (if required)
* 2½ cups (600ml) heavy (double) cream

Wild Notes

Use sweetened stoned damsons or sieved blackberries for wild and red ice cream.
Add Sweet Violet Syrup, page 38, and fresh sweet violets for violet ice cream, or infuse a custard-based ice cream overnight. Use with rose petals and rose syrup for rose ice cream.

Fruits & Berries

Fruits of the *Hedgerow* JAM

Unless foragers strike lucky, or have time available, their baskets are rarely full. However, foraging in Angus—raspberry country—I benefit from bird-carried raspberry seeds and can fill my basket with ease. Less fortunate foragers may have to top up with commerical berries, but the meadowsweet is essential and unavailable in the supermarket aisle.

What to do:

1 Wash the gooseberries and put them in a saucepan with the cordial, water, and meadowsweet heads. Bring to a boil, cover, and simmer until the gooseberries are soft, about 25 minutes.

2 Add the raspberries, and cook until the juices run.

3 Remove the meadowsweet heads and transfer the cooked fruit to a preserving pan.

4 Add the sugar, and cook over low heat to dissolve, stirring occasionally.

5 Bring the pan to a boil and boil rapidly until setting point is reached (see page 115)—about 15 minutes, but test after 12 minutes.

6 Skim off any scum and add a knob of butter to disperse any remaining scum. Ladle into warm, sterilized jam jars, cover with discs of waxed paper, and leave to cool. Store in a cool, dark place, and refrigerate after opening.

Makes 3–4 jars

What to forage and find:
* 4 cups (1 lb/450g) red gooseberries, topped and tailed
* 2 scant tablespoons meadowsweet cordial
* Scant ½ cup (100ml) water
* 2 meadowsweet heads, tied in a cheesecloth (muslin) bag
* 3½ cups (450g) wild raspberries
* 4½ cups (2 lb/900g) granulated sugar
* Knob of butter

Fruits & Berries

I make this in Kilner preserving jars, not bottles, because it's quite tricky to remove fruit (especially damsons and cherries) from narrow bottle necks—this recipe has a "Part Two" using the alcohol-soaked fruits in *Wild and Wicked After-Dinner Treats*, on page 122. However, if you are making *Sloe Gin* as a gift, use bottles.

Sloe Gin

Makes 8–9 small bottles
(3½ fl oz/100ml),
27–30 fl oz (800–900ml)
in total

What to forage and find:
* 1 lb (450g) softened by the frost (bletted), or frozen and defrosted, sloes (blackthorn berries)
* 1⅛ cups (225g) superfine (caster) sugar
* Approximately 2 cups (500ml) gin

What to do:
1 Sterilize a large jar in a dishwasher or oven.

2 Wash and dry the sloes, and prick them with a sharp fork or small knife, which will help release the juices. Defrosted sloes are usually pretty mushy, so if you are using these, you won't have to do this.

3 Fill the jar with the sloes, add the sugar, and pour in the gin, seal, and shake well. Store in a cool, dark place, but remember to give the jar a good shake on a daily basis for a couple of weeks. Then forget about it until Christmas at the very earliest (3–4 months). Ideally, leave it until next year.

4 Strain the ruby-red gin into a pitcher (jug) and then into sterilized, screw-topped bottle(s).

Wild Notes

Make this recipe with damsons and wild cherries, or replace the gin with vodka. A stick of cinnamon, or a star anise, adds flavor. For sweeter fruits (damsons), add less sugar. Cherry brandy using geans (wild cherries) and brandy can be made in the same way. When I make cherry brandy, I add a few drops of almond extract (essence) and 1 part sugar to 3 parts fruit.

Use the blossoms of sloes, wild cherries, and damsons to make syrup—see the recipe for Sweet Violet Syrup, page 38.

Fruits & Berries

121

Wild and *Wicked* After-Dinner Treats

This is a really wild "I-love-food-and-hate-waste" idea, using the alcohol-soaked berries from gins, vodka, and brandy—sheer indulgence.

Makes 15

What to forage and find:
* 3½ oz (100g) bittersweet (dark) chocolate (minimum 70% cocoa solids)
* ½ stick (50g) salted butter
* ¾ cup (100g) blanched almonds
* Pinch of dried red pepper flakes (crushed chilies)
* 3½ tablespoons (25g) sifted confectioners' (icing) sugar
* Generous ⅓ cup (50g) brandy-soaked wild cherries, pitted (stoned)

What to do:

1 Put the chocolate and butter into a bowl that fits snugly over a pan of simmering water, and stir until the mixture has melted. Remove from the heat.

2 Finely chop the almonds in a food processor, then add the pepper flakes (chilies) and confectioners' (icing) sugar, and blitz again.

3 Roughly chop the cherries.

4 Fold the almond mixture and cherries into the chocolate, and cool until the mixture is slow to return to the center of the bowl when moved to the edge with a spoon.

5 Spoon half of the mixture into the center of a piece of parchment paper, and carefully use the paper to shape it into a roll, about 6 inches (15cm) long. Fold the paper ends underneath, and put it on a baking sheet. Repeat with a second sheet of parchment paper, and the remaining mixture. Put the baking sheet in the refrigerator and leave to set for about 1½ hours. (Alternatively, roll the mixture into small balls.)

6 Cut into ⅜-inch (1cm) slices, and serve after a dinner as a delicious treat.

Wild Notes

Alternatively, you could use pitted, gin- or vodka-soaked sloes (fruit of the blackthorn), damsons, or hazelnuts, in place of the almonds. For added wild glitz, decorate the cut slices by pushing a tiny crystallized violet or rose petal into each cut slice.

You might also like to flambé wild fruits that have been used to make sloe gin, or vodka, or cherry brandy, and serve a spoonful on top of ice cream.

Fruits & Berries

122

CHAPTER 4

HERBS

About Sweet Cicely

Myrrhis odorata

"One morning in May
with dew on her face
Sweet Cicely looks up to see,
hovering above
declaring his love,
an elegant gentleman bee."
Alice Zucchini, Poems *About the Garden*

Colloquial names:

Aniseroot, Longstyle Sweetroot, Licorice Root, Wild Anise, Sweet-Hemlock, Sweets, The Roman Plant, Shepherd's Needle, Smooth Cicely, Cow Chervil

Where to find:

Sweet cicely grows by streams and on country lanes, with a tendency to lean on dry stone dykes or bridges as it dances in the breeze. It can grow up to 6 feet (2 metres) in height. If the downy, feathery leaves are bruised, the smell of aniseed is overwhelming. It reminds me of the French drink *Pastis*, which, as I usually forage in Scotland, brings with it an "Auld Alliance" smile. Spying the umbels of lacy, white flowers of sweet cicely is one of my early summer high points.

How to forage and gather:

Cut young leaves and regrowth is surprisingly fast. As with many plants, the leaves lose flavor when the flower blossoms. The late summer green seeds are one of my favorite wayside nibbles, and they dry well.

How to use:

Sweet cicely is a natural sweetener, and traditionally used to sweeten rhubarb, which is in season at the same time. Its hollow stems can be used as swizzle sticks for cocktails or straws for cordials, but do ensure that you don't confuse this sweet, aniseed-scented plant with hemlock. The stems of hemlock are hollow, too, but poisonous. The

sugar-saving properties of sweet cicely make it is a useful addition for the health-conscious cook. For those less worried about sugar, the stems can be candied, like angelica (which is available commercially). Angelica also has a dangerous resemblance to hemlock. For the confident, candied angelica is delicious, but the journey for the intrepid forager is best begun with candied sweet cicely, which is easily identified by its aniseed scent. The unusual seeds of sweet cicely are delicious in salads, or chopped in ice cream, and will add texture and flavor to stewed fruits. The roots taste of licorice. However, if you do forage roots, ensure that you have the landowner's permission. I don't gather any roots—in Scotland it is against the law to do so, unless you have been granted special permission.

A few leaves of sweet cicely can be added when steaming Brussels sprouts and greens, and they also work well in fish sauces. It is a natural partner for tart fruits. When dried, the flowers retain scent, and so lend themselves to infusion.

Sweet cicely seeds may be used in savory stir fries and salads or pickled, and the aniseed flavor works in cakes and puddings.

Folklore:

The Blackfeet (a Native American tribe) called sweet cicely "Paoh-coi-au-saukas," or "smell mouth." Their mares were given the herb to chew on, because it kept them in better condition when they were in foal. Native Americans made tea from sweet cicely, or chewed on the leaves, because it was thought to cure sore throats, coughs, and wounds.

The seeds of sweet cicely were used to polish furniture. I am rarely seen with a duster in hand, but perhaps I'll chance a quick wipe of the dining-room table with a bunch of sweet cicely; at the very least it will be a naturally scented, cleaning experience.

This recipe can be adapted for candied lovage and also angelica. Be wary of mistaking these for the poisonous hemlock, which was notoriously given to Socrates. The leaves of sweet cicely, when crushed, smell of aniseed; this is the safest option for beginners. If you do forage angelica, cut it in the spring, before the stems go pink, and choose thicker stems where possible.

CANDIED STEMS of *Sweet Cicely*

What to do:

1 Wash and trim the sweet cicely stems, and remove any loose strands. Soak the stems in a bowl of water for at least 6 hours, weighing the stems down with a plate to ensure that they remain submerged.

2 Put the sweet cicely stems in a pan, cover with boiling water, and add the baking soda (bicarbonate of soda). This will help the stems retain their color.

3 Cover and simmer until the stems begin to soften, about 45 minutes. Refresh the stems in cold water, and remove any loose, stringy pieces.

4 Heat the sugar and water in a pan over a low heat until the sugar has dissolved and boil rapidly for 1–2 minutes.

5 Add the prepared stems and boil for 2–3 minutes. Remove the pan from the heat. Allow the stems to cook briefly, and then put them on a cooling rack, with a tray underneath to catch drips. Leave to dry. Repeat step 5 over a 5-day period until the stems are translucent.

6 Remove the stems from the syrup with a slotted spoon. Keep the syrup to flavor and sweeten ice cream, fruit salads, or sauces. Put the stems on parchment paper, and leave them in a sunny window to dry completely, then cut them into smaller lengths (useful for decorating cakes). Store in an airtight container.

Makes 4½ oz (125g)

What to forage and find:
* Twelve 5½ x ⅜-inch (14 x 1cm) lengths of sweet cicely stems
* 1 tablespoon baking soda (bicarbonate of soda)
* 1¾ cups (400ml) water
* 4 cups (800g) superfine (caster) sugar

Wild Notes

Use the stems of angelica, lovage, or sweet cicely (before they become too big) as straws. Simply wash and trim them to size. The straws will add fun to summer picnics: use them for drinks, cold summer soups, or to add a wild buzz to a Virgin or Bloody Mary. Sweet cicely straws add a delicious taste of aniseed.

The prolonged sugar boiling will leave just a hint of aniseed in the candied stems. This recipe takes a long time from start to finish, but the resulting candied sweet cicely is well worth the effort.

Herbs

Wild Notes

Use sweetened young rhubarb juice with finely chopped sweet cicely to make a pink wobbly jelly the color of cotton candy (candy floss). All you need is some gelatin: a leaf (sheet) of gelatin will usually set ⅔ cup (150ml) liquid, but check the manufacturer's instructions. See Honeysuckle Jelly, page 24.

Sweet Cicely and RHUBARB SMOOTHIE

A delicious dusky pink, nutritious breakfast drink.

Serves 4

What to forage and find:

* 4–5 macadamia nuts (optional)
* 1 lb (450g) cooked rhubarb and sweet cicely (see *Sweet Cicely and Rhubarb Sorbet*, opposite)
* ¼ cup (25g) rolled (porridge) oats
* 2 tablespoons Greek (strained plain) yogurt
* ⅓–¾ cup (100–200ml) milk

What to do:

1 Roughly chop the macadamia nuts (if using) in a food processor.

2 Add the rest of the ingredients and process until smooth, adding milk until you reach your desired smoothie consistency. Sip the smoothies through sweet cicely straws.

Sweet Cicely and RHUBARB SORBET

The pinkness of tart young rhubarb stems in an icy marriage with sweet cicely is frozen deliciousness.

Serves 4

What to forage and find:
* 1 lb (450g) pink rhubarb
* 4–5 sweet cicely leaves
* ⅓ cup (75g) granulated sugar (to taste)
* Sugar syrup (*right*)

For the sugar syrup:
* Extra water (if required)
* ¾ cup (150g) granulated sugar
* 2 sweet cicely leaves, finely chopped

What to do:

1 Preheat the oven to 350°F (180°C/ gas mark 4).

2 Trim and cut the rhubarb into even-sized 1-inch (2.5cm) lengths, and put them in a colander. Rinse under cold, running water. Shake well, and put the rhubarb, sweet cicely leaves, and sugar in an ovenproof dish. Cover with foil and bake in the oven until the rhubarb is just soft, but retains its shape. Leave to cool.

3 When the rhubarb is cold, remove the sweet cicely, and strain off as much juice as possible.

4 For the sugar syrup, make the juice up to 1¼ cups (300ml) with water if necessary, and put this in a pan with ¾ cup (150g) granulated sugar. Simmer slowly to dissolve the sugar, then boil rapidly to reduce by half, 3–4 minutes. Leave to cool.

5 Blend the cold rhubarb and syrup in a food processor, and pour into a pitcher (jug). Add the finely chopped sweet cicely, stir well, then churn in an ice-cream machine until frozen.

Sweet Cicely COOKIES

Sweet cicely adds a very subtle taste to cookies.

Makes 24 cookies

What to forage and find:
* 1 stick +1 tablespoon (125g) unsalted butter, plus extra for greasing
* ¼ cup (50g) superfine (caster) sugar
* 1⅓ cups (180g) all-purpose (plain) flour
* Large handful (2½ tablespoons) finely chopped sweet cicely leaves
* 1 egg yolk

What to do:
1 Preheat the oven to 350°F (180°C/gas mark 4). Grease two baking sheets, or use nonstick baking sheets.

2 In a mixing bowl, cream the butter and sugar together.

3 Add the flour and sweet cicely leaves, and bind the mixture together with the egg yolk.

4 Knead the dough lightly, and divide in half. Roll into two 5 x 1½-inch (12 x 4cm) sausage-shaped rolls. Wrap each roll in plastic wrap (clingfilm), and refrigerate for at least 20 minutes.

5 Cut each roll into ⅜-inch (1cm) slices, and place them on the prepared baking sheets. Bake for about 12–15 minutes, until the cookies are lightly golden. Remove the baking sheets from the oven; leave the cookies to harden for 2–3 minutes, and then place on a cooling rack.

6 Store the cookies in an airtight tin.

Sweet Cicely SYRUP

Drizzle on ice cream or add a splash to a martini or gin, or just dilute with soda.

Makes 1¼ cups (300ml)

What to forage and find:
* 2 handfuls of sweet cicely leaves
* Generous ¾ cup (200ml) boiling water
* 1½ cups (300g) superfine (caster) sugar

What to do:
1 Put the sweet cicely leaves into a jam jar and add the boiling water. Cover and leave overnight.

2 The next day, strain the sweet cicely-infused water into a pan with the sugar. There will be about ⅔ cup (150ml), because the leaves will absorb water. Cook over very low heat to dissolve the sugar. DO NOT STIR. Bring the syrup to a boil briefly, and remove from the heat.

3 Pour the syrup into a pitcher (jug), cool briefly, remove any scum, then pour into a sterilized jam jar or small bottle.

For tips on making syrup, see *Sweet Violet Syrup, Wild Notes*, page 38.

Wild Notes
To crystallize sweet cicely flowers: dip a washed and dried flower into cold sweet cicely syrup, remove the flower, sprinkle with superfine (caster) sugar, and allow it to dry on parchment paper. Repeat the process three times. Store in an airtight tin, but ideally use as soon as possible.

Wild Blossom TEMPURA

Pick the sweet cicely flowers in sunshine with as long a stem as possible.

What to do:

1 Put the flour, egg, and sugar in a bowl and whisk until combined.

2 Gradually whisk in the sparkling water until you reach a thick batter consistency, which drops from the whisk slowly.

3 Hold the sweet cicely flowers by the stem, and dip in the batter until covered.

4 Heat the oil in a deep fryer until it reaches 350°F (180°C), and add the flowers in batches. Cook for about 2 minutes (depending on size). Keep cooked flowers warm in a low oven. Cover and label.

Makes 3 small jars

What to forage and find:
* 1 scant cup (125g) self-rising flour
* 1 egg, lightly beaten
* 1 tablespoon sweet cicely sugar, see *Flower and Herb Sugars and Salts*, page 15, or *Sweet Cicely Syrup*, opposite
* About ⅔ cup (150ml) cold sparkling water
* 20–25 sweet cicely flowers, attached to the stem

Wild Notes

Sweet cicely seeds can also be made into fritters: the cluster of seed heads is bigger, and you will use more tempura batter than you will if making blossom fritters. Serve with blossom sugars or syrups.

Replace the flower syrup or sugar with finely ground dried seaweed and pepper for a batter for sugar kelp tempura. Use 2-inch (5cm) square pieces of kelp (see *Sugar Kelp Crisps* recipe, page 172) and cook for 2½ minutes.

Herbs

About Jack-in-the-Hedge (Garlic Mustard)

Alliaria petiolata

"See-saw Jack in the Hedge,
Which is the way to London Bridge?
One foot up, the other foot down,
That is the way to London town."*
Mother Goose/Old Nursery Rhymes

Colloquial names:
Hedge Garlic, Jack-in-the-Bush, Lady's Needlework, Penny Hedge, Poor-Man's Mustard, Sauce-Alone

Where to find:
In shady, damp woodland, or hidden in hedgerows, away from the full glare of the sun. Closer to home, spy it in parks, wasteland, and gardens on the wild side.

This is a real spring green and can be found very early in the season, if the weather is kind. A second harvest can be gathered in a mild fall, but it is often tricky to find unless you can see the flowers. After the plants become "leggy," the leaves toughen.

The leaves closer to the top are the most tender. Growing in large groups, the larger leaves are heart-shaped, and the smaller (closer to the tip) are pointed, almost triangular. It can grow up to 3–6 feet (1–2 metres) tall. The white flowers (mid-spring to mid-summer) form in leafless clusters, each with four petals in the shape of the St. George cross. Bruise a leaf between your finger and thumb to release the lightest garlic aroma.

How to forage and gather:
Use scissors, and cut a few leaves from each plant. It is considered invasive in some areas of the US. Pick flowers for salads or decoration.

How to use:
Use in salads and sauces with as little cooking as possible because it loses its flavor when heated.

*Another version has "Boston" as the town instead of "London." You can find it in *The Heart of Oak Books, First Book* (1895) edited by Charles Eliot Norton.

Garlic Mustard and Chickweed Bruschettas

Uncooked hedgerow garlic maximizes the taste impact of this simple snack.

Wild Notes

Decorate with the segmented, small white flowers of garlic mustard (Jack-in-the Hedge). Alternatively, you can use the chopped stems of ramps (wild garlic) for a stronger flavor and added crunch.

Makes 15–20

What to forage and find:
* 4 ripe tomatoes, about 14 oz (400g)
* Zest of ½ small scrubbed orange
* 8-inch (20cm) portion French baton, or baguette, cut into 15–20 slices
* 1 tablespoon extra virgin olive oil
* 2 tablespoons washed and chopped garlic mustard (Jack-in-the-Hedge)
* 2 tablespoons washed and chopped chickweed
* Freshly ground black pepper

What to do:

1 Use a sharp knife to mark a small cross on each tomato and plunge the tomatoes in a bowl of boiling water for 10–15 seconds. Remove with a slotted spoon and plunge the tomatoes in cold water for 10 seconds. Remove the tomato skins.

2 Quarter the tomatoes and remove the seeds. Chop the flesh into small pieces and put it in a large sieve. Add the orange zest to the tomatoes. Leave to drain for at least 20 minutes.

3 Lightly toast the bread.

4 Put the drained tomatoes into a mixing bowl. Add the olive oil, chopped garlic mustard, and chickweed. Mix lightly, season with pepper, and, using a teaspoon, pile the mixture high onto the toasted bread.

Herbs

133

About Ramps (Wild Garlic)

Allium ursinum

Pedants argue a difference between British ramsons and US ramps but loosely, both may be referred to as wild garlic. English place names where wild garlic was prolific often contain the word "Rams." The place name and English surname Ramsdale are both likely derived from Ramsons. You may find three cornered leeks or indeed, few flowered leeks. Both can be used in wild garlic recipes but it isn't wild garlic.

Where to find:

It grows in damp woods, and shady places, and the smell is overwhelming. I associate it with early summer walks up a wooded bridle track to a Wiltshire Grammar school. Bluebells grew on one side of the track, and ramps on the other. First there was the pungent smell of garlic, then the pretty white flowers. The leaves are similar to the young leaves of "lords and ladies" (cuckoopint) and lily-of-the-valley, both of which are toxic, but there is no worry about confusion because the ramps leaves, when bruised, smell of garlic.

The white, star-shaped flowers hang in a dome of small umbels. The season is short; soon after flowering, wild garlic dies back—so it is a good idea to freeze or dry it.

How to forage and gather:

Frugally, unless there is an abundant supply, and use scissors to avoid tugging up the roots of smaller plants. The stalks, which are white earlier in the season, are quite delicious. I find the flavor more subtle and milder than the leaves. Another reason for cooking with the stalks is that leaves discolor with prolonged cooking. I have kept ramps wrapped in a plastic bag in the fridge for a week without adverse effect.

How to use:

Fresh: In salads, mayonnaise, butter, risottos, pasta sauces, and pesto, as a wrap for canapés, or with fish, lamb, and venison. In season, I use it in any recipe that calls for garlic.

Dried: If you have a food dehydrator, the leaves of ramps and garlic mustard can be dried and then crumbled by hand. Store in a jar and use a pinch out of season in stews and soups. Dried ramps is a wonderful addition to stuffing, and to herb crusts on meat and fish.

In oil: See *Ramps (Wild Garlic) Oil*, page 140, for juicing ramps and adding the juice to oil. The resulting emerald oil can be used in a multitude of ways: in bread, risottos, marinades, pasta, and root vegetable mash, but my favorite is a recipe for marinated olives. Immerse your olives in a mixture of ramps oil, and some herbs, and season well with freshly ground black pepper and sea salt, or even ramps flower salt, if you've made some.

Folklore:

There are records of ramps being used for a myriad of ailments, but my favorite has to be its use in the Scottish Highlands, where it was regarded as a "cure all"—mixed in butter with hawthorn blossom. One can't help wondering what they did from June to the following April (when it wasn't available).

Native Americans prized ramps too: the Cherokee Indians boiled or fried the plants, savoring its high vitamin content, and blood-cleansing properties.

Ramps (wild garlic) aioli is delicious with shellfish. Use eggs at room temperature, and add the oil trickle by trickle to prevent the mayonnaise curdling. The key to successful mayo is to work on a "go slow" basis.

Ramps (Wild Garlic) AIOLI

Makes 1¼ cups (300ml)

What to forage and find:
* 2 egg yolks
* Juice of 1 small lime
* Sea salt and freshly ground black pepper
* 1¼ cups (300ml) rice bran or other light vegetable oil
* 2 tablespoons finely shredded ramps (wild garlic) leaves
* *Ramps (Wild Garlic) Oil*, page 140 (optional)

What to do:
1 Put the egg yolks and lime juice into a bowl, season lightly, and whisk together.

2 Slowly whisk in the oil a little as possible at time, whisking constantly, until the oil has emulsified and the mayonnaise is thick. As the mayonnaise thickens, the oil can be added a little faster. If the mayonnaise looks very stiff, whisk in a little boiled water until the desired consistency is reached.

3 Fold in the shredded ramps and a drizzle of ramps oil if you have some.

4 Eat within 24 hours.

Wild Notes

If you have made ramps flower salt, use a pinch of this with some freshly ground black pepper. Alternatively, use garlic mustard (Jack-in-the-Hedge) instead of ramps.

I find a helping hand is useful when making mayonnaise; another adult, or child with a steady hand, pouring the oil in very slowly is really useful. You could make this in a food processor, but fold in the finely chopped ramps or garlic mustard by hand.

Elderflower Mayonnaise
This is delicious with steamed asparagus. Fold in a tablespoon of segments of elderflower blossom at Step 3 in place of the ramps.

Seaweed Mayonnaise
Fold in a teaspoon of dried sea lettuce, kelp, laver, or dulse at Step 3 in place of the ramps. Seaweed mayonnaise is delicious with freshly cooked langoustines.

Wild Watercress Mayonnaise
Fold in ½ cup (25g) of watercress, washed, dried, and finely chopped at Step 3 in place of the ramps.

Herbs

135

Minted Pea and *Ramps (Wild Garlic)* SOUP

What to do:

1 Wash and finely slice the ramps (wild garlic) stalks.

2 Heat the oil and butter in a saucepan and cook the ramps over low heat for 1 minute.

3 Cut the new potatoes into small pieces and cook with the ramps for another 1–2 minutes, stirring often.

4 Add 3½ cups (800ml) of the stock and bring to a boil. Cover the pan and simmer for 8–10 minutes until the potatoes are soft.

5 Add the peas and mint, and simmer for another 3 minutes to cook the peas.

6 Remove the pan from the heat, and allow it to cool for a minute.

7 Blend the peas and potatoes in a food processor, or with a hand blender, and return to the pan.

8 Use the remainder of the stock to rinse around the food processor bowl, and add enough to the saucepan to reach the desired consistency.

9 Heat over low heat to warm through, season with freshly ground pepper, and serve as soon as possible in warm bowls. Scatter ramps (wild garlic) flowers over the soup just prior to serving. If you wish, add a swirl of crème fraîche.

Serves 4

What to forage and find:
* 3½ oz (100g) ramps (wild garlic) stalks
* 1 tablespoon olive oil
* Knob of butter
* 10 oz (275g) scrubbed new potatoes
* 4½ cups (1 litre) vegetable stock
* 1 cup (150g) freshly shelled peas
* 3 mint leaves, finely shredded
* Freshly ground black pepper
* A handful of ramps (wild garlic) flowers

Herbs

Wild Notes

Decorate the soup with a
swirl of crème fraîche and
ramps (wild garlic) leaves
and flowers. For a really
minty soup, use mint tea
in place of stock, and a few
shredded mint leaves. On a
hot summer day, serve
this soup cold with ramps
ice cubes.

Wild Notes

If you've made ramps butter, you could use this in place of fresh leaves. You can replace the ramps with finely shredded garlic mustard (Jack-in-the-Hedge), or finely chopped few-flowered leeks.

New Potatoes in *Ramps* and Lemon

I cook this combination in late spring each year. Initially, its sheer simplicity made me question its inclusion in this book. However, where delicious seasonality marries the cultivated and wild in a few ingredients, it has to be a winner.

What to do:

1 Scrub the potatoes (to remove loose dirt). Valuable nutrients are just under the skin and these are lost in peeling. Cut any larger potatoes in half. Cook in a minimum quantity of boiling water for 15–20 minutes until the potatoes are just soft.

2 Meanwhile chiffonade the ramps leaves (roll the leaves up tightly and cut into thin shreds).

3 Drain and reserve the potatoes, and add the butter and lemon zest to the pan. Return to the heat briefly to melt the butter, then add the shredded ramps leaves. Cook for a minute to wilt the leaves, then return the potatoes to the pan.

4 Toss the potatoes in the butter, lemon, and ramps, and season with freshly ground pepper.

5 Turn into a warm serving bowl and scatter with tiny ramps flowers before serving.

Serves 4

What to forage and find:
* 1¾ lb (800g) new potatoes
* 8 ramps (wild garlic) leaves, washed and dried
* ¼ stick (25g) butter
* Zest of ½ lemon
* Freshly ground black pepper
* 2–3 ramps (wild garlic) flowers, washed, dried, and segmented

Herbs

New Potatoes *Ramps (Wild Garlic)* SALAD

The rusticity of scrubbed new potatoes and finely chopped wild garlic adds
to the provenance of this recipe, but a drizzle of wild garlic oil will impress.

What to forage and find:
* Ingredients as opposite
  with the addition of:
* 2 tablespoons crème
  fraîche
* A dash of lemon juice
* Ramps (wild garlic) oil
* 2–3 ramps and chive
  flowers, washed, dried,
  and segmented

What to do:

1 Use only half the amount of butter in the recipe opposite at Step 3
and let the potatoes cool completely.

2 Add the crème fraîche (or cream cheese mixed with light/single
cream) and a dash of lemon juice to the potatoes, and toss well.

3 Season with freshly ground pepper, then drizzle with emerald
green *Ramps (Wild Garlic) Oil* (page 140) and decorate with ramps
and chive flowers.

Wild Notes

You could also use the
flowers and leaves of finely
shredded garlic mustard
(Jack-in-the-Hedge).

Herbs

These mouthwatering homemade oatcakes are surprisingly easy to make. Once you've got to grips with the method, you can adapt the recipe to add dried seaweed or wild seeds or nuts in the fall.

Ramps (Wild Garlic) OATCAKES

What to do:
1 Preheat the oven to 190°F (375°C/ gas mark 5).

2 Melt the butter in a small pan over a low heat.

3 Sift the flour into a bowl and add the oatmeal, bicarbonate soda, salt and ramps. Add the melted butter and enough water to bind the mixture.

4 Turn the dough onto a work surface dusted with flour and roll out the dough to 3mm thickness. Cut the oatcakes into 2in. (5cm) rounds with a cookie cutter.

5 Pop the oatcakes onto a baking tray and bake for 20 minutes. Remove from the oven and turn onto a cooling rack.

Makes 15 small oatcakes

What to forage and find:
* 2oz (55g) butter
* 7 tablespoons (100g) all-purpose (plain) flour
* 2 scant cups (225g) medium oats (oatmeal), plus extra for sprinkling
* ½ teaspoon baking soda (bicarbonate of soda)
* ½ teaspoon salt
* 1 tablespoon finely chopped ramps (wild garlic) stalks
* 2–3 tablespoons lukewarm water

Ramps (Wild Garlic) OIL

One day I tried juicing ramps in a Magimix appliance, and I haven't looked back. This vibrant green oil is yummy, but should be used immediately, not stored.

What to do:
1 First make the ramps (wild garlic) juice. Wash the ramps leaves and stalks, and shake them dry (a few drops of water will aid the juicing).

2 Slowly push the leaves and stalks through an electric juicer.

3 Bottle and store in the fridge for up to 3-4 days or freeze in ice cube trays.

4 Mix one part ramps (wild garlic) juice to two parts oil for an amazing, vibrant green oil. Shake very well before use, and make small amounts as required. The effect of ramps oil drizzled over risottos and salads is spectacular. Ramps oil is especially delicious in a tomato and mozzarella salad.

Makes about ¼ cup (50ml)

What to forage and find:
* 5oz (150g) ramps (wild garlic)
* Extra virgin olive oil

Wild Notes

For a stronger flavor and color to the oatcakes, add some chopped ramps leaves.

Wild Rumbledethumps

Rumbledethumps is a Scottish recipe combining clapshot, the Orcadian dish of yellow turnips and potatoes, with another Celtic dish, colcannon from Ireland, which mixes potato with kale or cabbage. My "Wild Rumbledethumps" must also reference Pepys, who inspired me with his talk of "good nettle porridge."

Serves 4

What to do:

1 Preheat the oven to 375°F (190°C/ gas mark 5).

2 Peel and finely dice the potatoes and rutabagas (swede), steam until tender, and put into a bowl.

3 Heat the ramps (wild garlic) oil, and sauté the onions until soft. Add the finely chopped ramps stalks, and cook briefly.

4 Meanwhile, steam the nettle tops for 2–3 minutes, refresh in cold water, and squeeze well to remove excess water.

5 Add the butter to the hot root vegetables, and stir in the cooked onions, ramps, and nettles. Season well.

6 Turn the mixture into a greased ovenproof dish; use a knife to level the surface. Scatter the grated cheese and toasted oats over the top, and bake for 25–30 minutes until golden.

What to forage and find:

* ✳ 1¼ lb (600g) floury (baking variety) potatoes
* ✳ 12 oz (350g) rutabagas (swede)
* ✳ 2 tablespoons *Ramps (Wild Garlic) Oil*, page 140
* ✳ Large red onion, peeled and finely sliced
* ✳ 3½ oz (100g) ramps (wild garlic) stalks, washed and chopped
* ✳ 10½ oz (300g) nettle tops
* ✳ 5 tablespoons (75g) butter
* ✳ Sea salt and freshly ground black pepper
* ✳ ⅔ cup (75g) grated Cheddar cheese
* ✳ ¼ cup (25g) toasted rolled oats (oatmeal)— see *Wild Notes*, below

Wild Notes

To toast oats, put in a dry skillet (frying pan) and cook over medium heat, stirring occasionally, until golden. Store in an airtight container. Mix a pinch of dried sea lettuce into the pan when toasting oats for color, and a taste of the sea. Later in the year, use a clove of garlic and spinach instead of ramps stalks and nettles, and scatter toasted wild seeds over the cheese instead of oats.

Ramps (Wild Garlic) RAITZIKI

A refreshing wild dip or accompaniment for curry dishes.

Makes a small bowl

What to forage and find:
* ½ cucumber, peeled
* 1 teaspoon sea salt
* 15 chives, about 7 inches (18cm) in length
* 5 ramps (wild garlic), white stalks only, washed and dried
* 3 tablespoons reduced fat crème fraîche
* Zest and juice of ½ small lime
* Freshly ground black pepper

What to do:
1 Grate the cucumber into a sieve. Sprinkle with sea salt, and leave to drain for 10–15 minutes. Pat dry with paper towels (kitchen paper).

2 Chop the chives and ramps stalks very finely.

3 Put the crème fraîche into a small bowl. Add the well-drained cucumber, chives, ramps (wild garlic), lime zest and juice, and mix well. Season with freshly ground pepper.

Wild Notes

My husband, Stephen, invented this recipe name because it is a cross between a raita and a tzatziki. For a more intense flavor and color, add 2 teaspoons finely chopped ramps (wild garlic) leaves. You could also add chopped ramps stalks or leaves to paneer, guacamole, or hummus (see below).

Wild Hummus

In spring, go wild with hummus and guacamole by adding ramps (wild garlic), few-flowered leeks, or garlic mustard (Jack-in-the-Hedge). Hummus is one of my standby recipes: it's really just a question of mixing together a can of garbanzo beans (chickpeas), tahini (sesame paste), lemon juice, garlic, and oil. Consistency is a matter of taste.

Wild Notes

For extra color and texture, fold in 2–3 finely shredded ramps (wild garlic) leaves before putting the hummus into the bowl. Or you may prefer to add a heaping teaspoon of dried seaweed in place of the ramps.

What to do:
1 This is the easiest of recipes: simply put all of the ingredients into a food processor except for the olive oil and ramps oil, and then blend.

2 Add olive oil until the desired consistency is reached and turn into a serving dish. Make a dip in the center and swirl a little ramps (wild garlic) oil in the dip.

3 Serve with warm pita (pitta) bread, crudités, or as a dip or sandwich spread.

Makes 1 bowl

What to forage and find:
* 14 oz (400g) canned (tinned) chickpeas
* Lemon zest and juice
* 1 tablespoon light tahini
* 2 ½ oz (about 10 lady's handfuls/75g) ramps (wild garlic) stalks, washed
* About a scant ½ cup (100ml) extra-virgin olive oil
* *Ramps (Wild Garlic) Oil*, page 140

Ramps (Wild Garlic) BREAD

Ramps (wild garlic) and dairy products will for many people be synonymous with Thomas Hardy's wonderful story, *Tess of the d'Urbervilles*. This recipe uses ramps in the bread, but you could gild the bread with *Ramps (Wild Garlic) Butter* too, page 148.

Makes 1 flat circular loaf

What to forage and find:
* 3½ cups (500g) white bread (strong white) flour, plus extra for dusting
* 1¼-oz envelope active dry yeast (7g sachet fast action yeast)
* 1 teaspoon ramps salt, page 15
* 2 tablespoons *Ramps (Wild Garlic) Oil*, page 140
* 2 tablespoons finely chopped ramps stalks
* Approximately 1 cup (225ml) lukewarm water

For the top of the loaf:
* 1 teaspoon ramps salt
* 2 teaspoons ramps oil

What to do:

1 Preheat the oven to 450°F (230°C/gas mark 8).

2 Put the flour into a bowl with the yeast, salt, oil, chopped ramps stalks, and enough water to make a soft dough.

3 Knead on a lightly floured surface for about 10 minutes, until the dough is springy and elastic.

4 Put the dough into a lightly floured bowl, cover with plastic wrap (clingfilm) or a large plastic bag, and leave to rise in a warm place for about an hour, until the dough has doubled in size.*

5 On a baking sheet, shape the dough into a circular loaf, and use a thumb to dimple the top of the dough. Cover again and leave for 15 minutes.

6 Stretch to shape, and dimple again. Sprinkle with the ramps salt, and drizzle the oil over the top.

7 Place a small metal dish of water in the preheated oven, and bake the bread at 450°F (230°C/gas mark 8) for 10 minutes, then for a further 45 minutes at 375°F (190°C/gas mark 5). Tap the base to ensure it sounds hollow (to test that the bread is baked.) Wrap in a kitchen (tea) towel, and leave to cool on a rack.

Wild Notes

If you add finely shredded ramps (wild garlic) leaves to bread, although the leaves will discolor during baking, the bread will have an intense garlic flavor. Olive oil and sea salt can replace the ramps oil and salt, but add an extra tablespoon of chopped stalks.

About Wild Thyme

Thymus serpyllum

Where to find:
This aromatic herb with small purple flowers is found on sand dunes, grassland, rocks, and moors. It spreads itself like a carpet, and to wander upon it barefoot is a wonderful experience—aromatherapy for the feet. I wasn't surprised to read that the Greeks and Romans used it for bathing.

How to forage and gather:
Wild thyme can be found from late spring to early fall. Cut the stems with scissors and remove the leaves later. The flowers have a lovely flavor, too.

How to use:
Wild thyme has a milder flavor than garden thyme, so you may need to add a little more. The tiny, oval-shaped leaves are delicious in both savory and sweet dishes. Try scattering some leaves over a ham before roasting it in

Wild Thyme PUFFS

Delicious served with *Quince and Wild Thyme Sorbet*, page 109.

Makes 15

What to forage and find:
* 1 scant cup (100g) finely grated Parmesan cheese
* 1 tablespoon chopped wild thyme

What to do:
1 Preheat the oven to 350°F (180°C/gas mark 4).

2 Mix the Parmesan cheese and wild thyme together in a bowl.

3 Line a baking sheet with parchment paper, and heap the cheese and wild thyme mixture onto it in rough 2¼-inch (6cm) circles (½-inch/1cm high), leaving space in between, because the crisps will spread.

4 Bake for 5 minutes, or until the cheese is golden. Leave on the baking sheet to harden for a few minutes, then remove the crisps with a spatula (palette knife).

Wild Notes

Replace the wild thyme with other shredded wild leaves: lovage, ramps (wild garlic), wild marjoram, or bog myrtle, or a teaspoon of dried sea lettuce or dulse.

Herbs

About Scots Lovage

Ligusticum scoticum

Where to find:
On shingle above the high-tide line, and on rocky infertile soil.

How to forage and gather:
Gather seeds in fall, in moderation. Snip the leaves with scissors.

How to use:
The large, trefoil-shaped leaves are reminiscent of celery, and should be used sparingly—a wipe around a salad bowl will be sufficient. They can be used in salads, soups, and also when cooking venison or other strong meats. The stems are hollow, and make interesting "celery-flavored" straws for drinks; try one with tomato juice, or cold gazpacho soup. Lovage is purported to help scurvy and was given to long-suffering sailors on their return from voyages.

QUINOA with *Lovage-infused* Chicken

Quinoa is an ancient grain from the Andes, and was one of the staple foods of the Incas. It is high in protein, and easy to prepare.

Serves 3–4

What to forage and find:
* 7 oz (200g) young nettle leaves
* 9 oz (250g) chicken breast
* 2–3 black peppercorns
* 3 lovage leaves
* Scant 1¼ cups (200g) quinoa
* 4 teaspoons ground roasted coriander and cumin (see right)
* Large ripe avocado
* 1 teaspoon lemon juice
* 1 tablespoon extra virgin olive oil
* Lemon wedges to garnish

What to do:
1 Blanch the nettle leaves in boiling water for 30 seconds, and refresh in cold water. Drain very well.

2 Put the chicken, peppercorns, and lovage in a saucepan, and cover with water. Bring the water to a boil, and simmer for 10–15 minutes until the chicken is cooked and the juices run clear when tested. Remove the chicken and reserve the stock. Discard the lovage and peppercorns.

3 Rinse the quinoa well, and pat dry. Put it into a skillet (frying pan) with a teaspoon of roasted coriander and cumin*; dry roast for 3–4 minutes, turning frequently until the quinoa is lightly browned.

4 Transfer the quinoa to a saucepan, and add enough reserved chicken stock to cover. Be careful, the quinoa retains heat after dry-roasting. Bring to a boil, and simmer for 10 minutes. Drain very well, and turn the quinoa into a bowl. Add the nettle leaves to the hot quinoa, stir gently, and leave to cool.

5 Slice the chicken breast thinly, and add to the quinoa and nettles. Roughly chop the avocado flesh, and add this with the remaining roasted spices, lemon juice, and oil to the quinoa, and gently toss everything together.

* Dry-roast cumin and coriander seeds in a skillet (frying pan) until golden and then grind in a pestle and mortar.

BUTTER with *Wild Leaves, Herbs, Seaweeds*

I often fill a Victoria sandwich cake with a floral butter, or butter mixed with a fruit curd. My excuse is that I love the rich taste of butter. Its natural creaminess can be enhanced by the addition of wild ingredients, including herbs, leaves, and seaweeds.

Ramps (Wild Garlic) Butter

Makes a scant ½ cup (100g)

What to forage and find:
* 1 stick minus 1 tablespoon (100g) butter
* 3–4 ramps (wild garlic) leaves, washed and dried
* Pinch of ramps (wild garlic) salt (optional)

What to do:

1 Bring the butter to room temperature, and put it in a bowl.

2 Shred the washed and dried wild garlic leaves by rolling them as tightly as you can, and then chopping finely.

3 Add the shredded ramps to the butter (with the wild garlic salt if using,) and use a fork to mash it together. Refrigerate until firm.

Douglas Fir Butter

Makes 1 small bowl

What to forage and find:
* 1 stick (125g) butter
* Heaping teaspoon ground Douglas fir needles

What to do:

1 Bring the butter to room temperature in a small bowl.

2 Mix in the ground Douglas fir needles and refrigerate until firm.

> ### *Wild Notes*
> Use ramps (wild garlic) butter in garlic bread recipes, with new or baked potatoes, mashed root vegetables, pressed under the skin of roast chicken, as a base for a roux, or to cook omelets, scrambled eggs, and other egg-based dishes.
> Bog myrtle or wild thyme can replace Douglas fir needles in chicken and fish recipes.

Seaweed Butter

Makes a scant ½ cup (100g)

What to forage and find:
* 1 stick (125g) butter
* 2 teaspoons dried sea lettuce

What to do:

1 Bring the butter to room temperature, and put it into a food processor.

2 Add the sea lettuce, and turn the machine to low speed, until the seaweed is evenly distributed through the butter. Alternatively, mash the soft seaweed butter with a fork or potato masher.

3 The original shelf life of the butter remains the same. You may like to try dried dulse, kelp, or laver in place of sea lettuce.

About Borage

Borago officinalis

Colloquial names:
Burrage, Talewort, Bugloss, Starflower, Herb of Gladness, Cool Tankard

Where to find:
Borage readily self-seeds and will return on an annual basis. It is an escapee from old gardens, and often found on rubbish heaps and in woodlands and pastures. This stunning flower has five petals that fold back to resemble a star, clustered around a black, peaked center. The petals vary from blue through violet pinks to white, while the dull leaves are hairy, almost prickly.

How to forage and gather:
Gather the leaves before the plant comes into flower, and blossoms for crystallizing on a sunny day. To dry, spread leaves on a sunny windowsill where air circulates or in a dehydrator.

How to use:
The flowers can be added to conserves (just before the end of the rolling boil) or crystallized and used to decorate cakes. The leaves, which taste delicious and are reminiscent of cucumber, are often served in summer drinks. In bygone days, before refrigerators, they were added to claret cups and ales for a cooling effect. A few borage leaves add flavor to summer greens, and they can be eaten raw in salads, spreads, and dips, and in pesto. Add finely chopped young borage stems to soups and casseroles, and use the dried leaves in tisanes.

To make 12 borage ice cubes, find 12 pink, white, or blue star-shaped borage flowers and put them in an ice tray. Cover with water (be careful not to overflow because the flowers will float to the top) and freeze. Borage flowers traditionally add summer color to Pimms, and brighten up cordials and cocktails.

Borage and CASHEW PASTE

Use to stuff lamb, fish, or chicken, in sandwiches, or with pasta.

Makes a small bowlful

What to forage and find:
* 4 cups (75g) young borage leaves, stalks removed
* Scant ½ cup (50g) cashew nuts, toasted in an oven or dry skillet (frying pan)
* 1 clove garlic, crushed
* ½ cup (30g) finely grated Parmesan cheese
* Pinch of sea salt
* Grated zest and juice of ½ lemon
* About ½ cup (125ml) olive oil

What to do:
1 Wash the borage leaves and pat them dry.

2 Place all of the ingredients except the oil in a food processor and whiz briefly to blend.

3 With the motor running, add enough oil to form a thick paste.

Wild Notes
In spring, use washed and well-dried ramps (wild garlic) stalks in place of the garlic clove.

Herbs

149

CHAPTER 5

SEA *and* *Shore*

The Seaweed Collection

Marine Algae

The Outer Hebrides has a seaweed tradition that, with Ireland, differs from the rest of the UK. Seaweed has always been a part of the way of life here: from farming on the *machair* (fertile plains) to cooking in the kitchen. Nineteenth-century immigrants took this passion, especially for dulse and carrageen, with them to North America. There are hundreds of species of seaweeds, and many of them are delicious raw, cooked, or dried. I mention a mere handful in this book, but those used are relatively easy to identify, and a good place to begin a seashore foray. All marine algae are saltwater plants, i.e. they grow and are nourished in salt water. They don't have roots, but a "holdfast"—seaweed fronds (leaves) are attached to the holdfast by a stipe (stalk). The job of the holdfast is, as its name suggests, to keep the seaweed firmly rooted in one place, even in storms. Seaweeds are grouped by color and different species are found in each tidal zone. Some grow on each other (epiphytes). Many seaweeds are kitchen chameleons, changing color when cooked. Unlike fungi, seaweeds are not toxic, although some are tastier than others.

Seaweed is rich in minerals and vitamins, and is very versatile in the kitchen. You may have eaten it without realizing—carrageen is a natural setting agent, used commercially. If properly managed, the potential of seaweed is enormous. It is a renewable source that research suggests has many nutritional benefits. Seaweed might be described often as green and slimy, but there are in fact more brown and red species of seaweed than green, and the current news is it's good for you.

Tides:

The alignment of the earth with the sun and moon is important for the seaweed forager, who will come to understand spring and neap tides, and when it is best to harvest seaweed—after a spring tide (approximately every 2 weeks).

Tides "rise" rather than "come in and out", and as the tide rises, it covers more land, dependent on the land's slope. The difference between high and low tide is the tidal range, and this is important knowledge for the seaweed collector. There is a greater tidal range during spring tides than neap tides. Naturally, not all of the seabed is instantly exposed by a falling tide; it takes about 6 hours and 12 minutes for each tide to fall, and then it starts to rise again, taking another 6 hours and 12 minutes. Thus the time between successive high tides is, on average, about 12 hours and 25 minutes.

Coastal zones:

The shore is divided into zones, and some understanding of them is important for seaweed collection. Zones are more distinguishable on rocky than sandy beaches.

Upper Shore (or Splash Zone)

In a tidal cycle, the first part of the seabed to be exposed is that farthest up the shore. This area will not be covered by water again until the next high tide in 10–12 hours' time; so anything that grows here has to withstand long periods of drying out (dessication) after being saturated in seawater.

Middle Shore (or Intertidal Zone)

This is about halfway between high and low water marks: the seabed will be uncovered for roughly 5–7 hours, half each tidal cycle. Some exposure occurs here, but conditions are less extreme than on the upper shore. This is where you find rock pools.

Lower Shore (or Subtidal Zone)

This area, close to the low-water mark, is exposed for just a short time, a couple of hours at most. This is where it all happens for the seaweed and shellfish forager, but harvesting must be swift—the tide waits for no man.

The Browns

Kelps are the flavor enhancers. In Scotland, "kelp" originally referred to the ash from burnt seaweeds, formerly used to make glass and soap.

Oar Weed
Laminaria digitata

Forest Kelp
Laminaria hyperborea

Sugar Kelp
Saccharina latissima

Colloquial names:
Oar weed: Tangle Kelp, Sea Ribbon, Kombu (Japan)
Forest Kelp: Sea Rods, May Weed
Sugar Kelp: Poor Man's Weatherglass, Sea Belt, Kombu Royale

Where to find:
Oar weed and forest kelp are very similar but the stipe of the latter is usually thicker and circular, not oval (as is the case with oar weed) in cross-section i.e. when cut in half. You will often find dulse growing (as an epiphyte) on forest kelp. Sugar kelp is a brown seaweed, which was traditionally used to forecast the weather, hence its local name poor man's weather vane or .

The stipe of oar weed is smooth and flexible, while forest kelp's stipe is rough. These kelps are orderly, first you'll come across oar weed and as you go deeper out to sea, the oar weed is replaced by forest kelp. The holdfast anchors on rocks and small pebbles.

Coco, our dog, likes us to throw forest kelp stipes for her to bring back from the sea—they are almost stick-like.

How to forage and gather:
I wear my pink wetsuit to forage kelps in clear, but cold, Hebridean seas. You don't need a boat; just be prepared to get a wee bit wet. Harvest from spring to fall, on the lower shore. Sugar kelp has a very short stipe, and is easily pulled away from rocks by storms. DO NOT COOK with storm cast seaweed i.e. seaweed lying on the beach. Use scissors to cut fresh seaweed from well above its holdfast.

How to use:
Kelp is nutrient packed and in its dried form is very versatile. Sprinkle as you cook and use it as an alternative to salt. Oar weed kelp is used in Japanese cooking as a natural form of monosodium glutamate (MSG). Its addition is rumored to speed up the cooking time of pulses.

TOP TO BOTTOM:
Forest kelp, oar weed, sugar kelp
OPPOSITE: Foraging on the seashore.

The Reds

Carrageen
Chrondus crispus
Mastocarpus stellatus

Colloquial names:
Irish Moss, E407, E407a (when used in food products)
Grape Pip Weed

Where to find:
For me, carrageen is the prettiest of the seaweeds. Found on the lower shore, it is a rich, red algae with flexible fronds that vary in shape and color from brown to green to purple, and even white. Grape pip weed is rather bristly to the touch and often covered in bubbly warts. *Chrondus crispus* is smoother.

How to forage and gather:
It is available all year but best picked from spring to fall at low tides. It is attached to rocks or pebbles by a short stalk. Use scissors to cut carrageen high up its short stipe (stalk), as far from the holdfast as possible.

How to use:
Carrageen sets well when combined with milk products but, in my experience, more is needed for setting wild cordial jellies. Prannie Rhatigan suggests that boiling carrageen in the presence of acid alters its structure, so add lemon or lime to cooled carrageen. In the Hebrides, it was used in a jelly drink (a thick liquid, not set) and Mrs Beeton (*Book of Household Management*) talks of it in invalid's drinks. Seaweed is rich in vitamins, a fact much appreciated by our ancestors.

Dulse
Palmaria palmata

Colloquial names:
Dillisk, Duileasc

Where to find:
On the middle and lower shore, but often hitches a ride on kelp or other seaweeds. The frond is up to 12 inches (30cm), usually with five tough, "finger-like" lobes.

How to forage and gather:
Cut dulse with a knife or scissors, well above its holdfast.

How to use:
Dulse can be used as other seaweeds, in fresh, dried, or rehydrated form. The taste of dried dulse (as with other seaweeds) is concentrated, so less is more. Historically dulse, both fresh and dried, was used as chewing gum—it is much healthier for you than tobacco.

TOP: *Carrageen*
ABOVE: *Dulse*

The Greens

Sea Lettuce
Ulva lactuca

Where to find:
Attached to rocks or other seaweeds on the middle as well as the lower shore.

How to forage and gather:
This is one of my favorite seaweeds, and it is easy peasy to forage. It looks like round salad lettuce, and is pale green when young, and a vivid emerald green when mature. The single-layered, crumpled fronds are delicate, almost paper-like. Sea lettuce and other Ulva spp. (e.g. gutweed or sea grass) like human effluence so don't forage this near drains on the upper shore. It is best picked at low tide in rock pools on the middle to lower shore. The Ulva spp. retain color when cooked, so they are useful but they have a strong taste of the sea, so use sparingly. The flavor is more subtle when baked.

How to use:
Sea lettuce dries with ease, retains its color on cooking, even in a deep fryer (*Scotch Quail Eggs with Sea Lettuce*, page 166). And for the lazy cook who likes to "wrap," it's nature's answer to parchment paper (cooking *en papillote*).

Marsh Samphire
Salicornia europaea

Colloquial names:
Glasswort, Sea Asparagus, Sampiere, Sea Fennel, Sea Beans

Where to find:
Marsh samphire, as the name suggests, is found on mud flats and estuaries below the high tide mark.

How to forage and gather:
Richard Mabey writes that the best specimens of marsh samphire are washed by every tide. Use scissors to pick the tips, and avoid the roots. As the season progresses, the stems can become woody, so allow for some wastage when preparing recipes. Marsh samphire is increasingly hard to find, so foragers should be mindful of overpicking. Marsh samphire should not be confused with rock samphire (*Crithmum maritimum*), which is also increasingly tricky to find in the UK. Both species should be foraged sustainably.

How to use:
Marsh samphire is an emerald green, fleshy plant, which bursts with "seaside" juice. If you come across samphire on a beach, when you are picnicking, put some in a sandwich and taste the sea—it's a far more zingy salt fix than bacon, and works just as well with chorizo and ham as in egg or fish sandwiches. Samphire is delicious raw, and may also be steamed, lightly boiled, or stir-fried. In recipes, it marries well with fish and lamb, but my favorite way to eat it is simplicity itself—in an omelet; you might add smoked salmon for a special occasion. There is a tradition of pickling samphire (see *Pickled Dulse*, page 173).

ABOVE: *Marsh samphire*

Sea Kale
Crambe maritima

Colloquial name:
Scurvy Grass, Sea Cabbage

Where to find:
Sea kale is found on cliffs, among sand dunes, and on the beach (at the top of the shoreline of shingle beaches). The larger lower leaves are crinkly, and the upper leaves smaller. From late spring to late summer, the small white flowers are magnificent, but it's the naturally sand- or shingle-blanched stalks that are considered a delicacy.

How to forage and gather:
I pondered over the inclusion of sea kale because it is scarce. You can buy cultivated sea kale, and I think that this would be a more sustainable option than to cook with foraged. Spy on sea kale in the wild and delight in so doing, but do not pick it unless it is prolific and a few delectable stalks won't be missed. Some foragers can be very restrained on their local patch, but yet content to plunder more distant neighborhoods. The local foraging habit, a "pick and come again" idea, is exactly how we should all forage wherever we are. The young stalks are eaten before the leaves have really developed. Pick the stems in spring and the flowers in summer.

How to use:
Sea kale can be pickled but its flavor is so delicate I fear vinegar would be a bully. I treat it like asparagus—a vegetable king that can stand alone. If you are lucky enough to find sea kale in plentiful bloom, try a flower for a taste of seaside sweetness.

Sea Arugula (Sea Rocket)
Cakile maritima

Where to find:
Sea arugula, unlike sea kale, is plentiful.

How to forage and gather:
Pick sea arugula in spring and summer. It is an acquired taste, so forage with abandon because not many other folk will follow in your footsteps.

How to use:
Steaming or blanching removes some of the pungency, but use it carefully: less is definitely more. Sea arugula is in flower all summer, and I find the pinkish purple flowers more palatable than the leaves. The younger leaves can be served in a salad. The leaves are fleshy to enable them to retain moisture when sand is blown over them. The pink flower infused in rice vinegar adds color and peppery flavor. This is my favorite way to use sea rocket.

TOP LEFT: *Sea kale*
BELOW: *Sea arugula (sea rocket)*
OPPOSITE: *Foraging in shallow water.*

How to gather seaweed:

Gather at low tide when submerged plants come within easy reach. The best place to look for seaweed is along rocky shores, because seaweed needs to grip on to something, even if it is only a small pebble. You will find seaweed that has been thrown up by stormy seas along the tide line of sandy beaches but you should not cook with storm cast seaweed. A different plastic bag for each variety you collect is useful, and this avoids any sorting when you return home. Place a small pebble in each bag, so that it doesn't blow away as you forage.

Ensure that you are clad in suitably warm and waterproof attire. I have a pink wetsuit, in season gold jelly shoes, and for colder weather, warm purple rain (wellington) boots. Waterproof boots with decent grips are useful on colder days, as are non-slip soles in summer for clambering over rocks. A pair of neoprene gloves will avoid freezing cold hands, and novice foragers should take a pocket reference book to help with seaweed I.D. Strong scissors or a small knife are helpful, too.

Respect marine wildlife:

Many small crustaceans and other creatures live in the sheltered rocks and holdfasts of seaweed; try not to disturb them, and shake harvested seaweed well to enable any residents to relocate in the locality.

Don't remove the seaweed stalks (stipes). If the modern seaweed industry uses machines to rip the stipes from the seabed, the sustainability of seaweed may be in question, but careful, hand harvesting of seaweed should have little impact on the seaweed population.

Don't cut through the holdfast and leave plenty behind; forage the length of the beach and replace any rocks that you peep under. This message is the same when foraging shellfish. Leave behind nothing but your footprints

How to dry seaweed:

Food Dehydrator: Sometimes the obvious is staring you in the face and you don't see it. My Hebridean clothes line (washing line) was full of seaweed and I was mumbling about sun and natural seaweed drying, when Alasdair, son number three, said, "Mum, what about using the food dehydrator?" I haven't looked back, and if you are a serious seaweed forager (or even a serious forager), the expenditure is well worthwhile.

Sea lettuce will dry within a few hours; thicker kelps may take longer, depending on the thickness of the frond. As with foraging, less is more; don't overload the trays of the dehydrator.

Low Oven: This can be tricky unless your oven can be set to a very low temperature, and I tend to need to leave the door open, which isn't very cost-effective.

Hot Oven: This works relatively well, providing the phone doesn't ring, and you have the oven on anyway (perhaps for making bread), and are prepared to watch the seaweed carefully; it burns easily.

On the Stovetop (Hob): Dry the seaweed as you would dry-roast spices or oatmeal: with a watchful eye, and stirring frequently.

On a Clothes Line (Washing Line) and/or a Sunny Windowsill: exact timing is climate dependent.

Storage: Store dried seaweed in an airtight container. It can be stored in large pieces, or ground before storing. Keep seaweed dry; dulse in particular has a tendency to absorb any moisture, and often retains a chewy texture.

How to grind seaweed:

* Place it in a sealed plastic bag and bash it with a rolling pin.
* Use a small food processor.
* Grind it in small quantities in a mortar and pestle, or a coffee grinder.

About Shellfish and Molluscs

There are many more shellfish than those mentioned in the recipes here. I have avoided foraging for any that require a line net (prawns or shrimp), a hook (crab), or pot (lobster). I've called them the molluscs and included only the "gourmands," not winkles, dog whelks, or limpets.

Safety first:
As I write, there has been an outbreak of shellfish food poisoning on Benbecula (Outer Hebrides)—a potential worry for foragers, and a reason why many folk avoid gathering shellfish. Only eat shellfish that have fully opened after cooking.

Laws about the collection of shellfish vary, so check local ownership. In the UK, for example, freshwater mussels are an endangered species and should not be foraged anywhere. However, laws for sea-mussel foragers differ from country to country. The quality of water is important. Do not collect from polluted waters (where sewage overflows or beaches are littered), and adhere to law-enforced restrictions imposed due to health warnings.

There is an old British adage not to eat shellfish when there isn't an "r" in the month. This is NOT an old wives' tale—apparently, the amount of bacteria found in shellfish between May and August, i.e. late spring until late summer, is significantly higher than at other times.

Before cooking, soak shellfish in salted water. Clams (cockles) will to some extent clean themselves, but this is not equivalent to a tightly controlled depuration process. The danger comes principally from the shellfish's filtration system. Unlike crustaceans (such as crabs, shrimps, and lobsters), molluscans obtain nutrients by pumping seawater through their gills, and filtering out tiny organisms, which are then ingested. While so doing, they can take in bacteria, viruses, and chemicals, and these become concentrated in their bodies. If shellfish aren't cooked (and the contaminants killed or neutralized as a consequence), they can make people sick. Eating raw shellfish is risky; cooking usually kills bacteria and viruses.

Store shellfish in seawater, not tap water, and use as soon as possible. Check that shellfish are alive before cooking—they can be frozen briefly so that they are dormant when cooked. Eat only shellfish that are fully open after cooking. Cook in small pans to ensure even cooking time.

Mussels
Mytilus edulis

Where to find:
There is an outer Hebridean beach where, when the tide is out, you can see a tractor clad in mussels; rusty metal discarded by man providing residency for members of the mollusc family. Large areas of this beach, when exposed at low tide, are black with colonies of mussel shells. Mussels are found on wave-washed rocks and may be harvested at low tide. A fast-moving tide probably ensures that there is less risk of pollution. Summer mussels are often underweight, and may be at risk of bacterial pollution in the warmer months. Check any local minimal harvesting mussel or clam size.

How to forage and gather:
Harvesting mussels is simple: twist larger ones free from rocks, and put them into a bucket. Once home, wash the mussels well under running water, and remove the beard (the brown, wispy hairs at the joint of the shell that anchored the mussel to the rock). This is arduous, but a good tug using a knife is helpful—wild mussel beards can be tough. Our youngest son, Maxim, was once caught shaving the mussels' beards with his father's razor—it worked. I am not too fussed by barnacles, but if you are, begin the tedious task of removing them. Some folk suggest adding a handful of oatmeal to a bucket of mussels in salted water, to aid cleaning.

How to use:

Steam or simmer mussels and discard any that fail to open during cooking. Cooked mussels can be added to fish pies and pasta dishes but beware of overcooking—they become rubbery.

Clams
Mercenaria mercenaria

Cockles
Cerastoderma edule

Where to find:

Forage at low tide in estuaries and sheltered sandy bays.

How to forage and gather:

Clam digging (US) and cockling (UK) is a fun family pastime. Mussels can be foraged with ease, but are tricky to clean, whereas clamming (cockling) can take time to fill the bucket with a decent number for supper, but the clams and cockles will clean themselves. Hydraulic dredgers often harvest commercially collected clams and cockles, but I often see Hebrideans filling cockling baskets with just a rake to aid them. Small children can use a sandbox rake, or beach pail and shovel (bucket and spade) to hunt their clams/cockles. They hide just a few inches (centimeters) under the sand. A quick muddy sand kick can throw up a cockle or two, and the exercise is good, too. Hands can be useful, if you don't mind nails full of sand, but a garden rake will ensure the fullest bucket. Move around the beach as you clam/cockle—spread your foraging evenly. Don't leave heaps of mud behind you; this disturbs other wildlife. Be aware of local regulations, the spawning season, and the minimum size of clam or cockle that can be harvested. Tides can be dangerous; it is easy to become stranded.

How to use:

Soak clams/cockles overnight in salted water and they will clean themselves, although some grit usually remains. As with mussels, check that cockles are alive before cooking them, and do not eat any that fail to open when cooked. Use as mussels, or pickle them.

Razor Clams
Ensis ensis, Ensis siliqua, Solen marginatus, Ensis arcuatus

There are four common razor clams, the shells of which resemble an old-fashioned barber's razor. A long "foot" enables the razor clam to move through the sand rather like a knife. Tempting one up from the sand can take time, but catching one is an exhilarating experience. As with other shellfish, avoid the summer months.

Where to find:

Forage at low tide in estuaries and sheltered sandy bays.

How to forage and gather:

One way of enticing a razor clam up to the surface is to sprinkle salt over the 'keyhole' visiting cards left in the sand by the razor clam. I've had varying degrees of success, affected by wind and temperature. Find a beach strewn with razor clamshells on a wind-free day. The telltale secret of razor clam presence is a small slit in the sand, betraying activity below. Squirt saline solution or salt over the hole and stand back; with HUGE luck, the next step is quick, if you have enticed a razor clam to the surface—grab it. Take care because the edge of the shell is sharp—it is all in the name—razor.

How to use:

Razor clams, once removed from their shells, may be eaten in their entirety—intestines too. The meat is white and tender when cooked.

TOP TO BOTTOM: *Razor clams, clams, cockles*
OPPOSITE: *Mussels*

Cashew and *Dulse* PRALINE

Dulse is one of my foraging delights—it hitches a ride on kelp on my local beach. At times, my boys describe the beach as "kelp rotting stinky," but it's worth wandering out at low tide to find "dulse hands" woven around kelp stipes. This recipe marries dulse with cashews; add some dried kelp ribbons if you like.

Makes 1 small bowlful

What to forage and find:
* handful fresh dulse, roughly chopped
* ⅔ cup (150ml) boiling water
* ⅔ cup (75g) cashew nuts
* tablespoon dried, finely ground dulse
* 1½ cups (300g) granulated sugar

What to do:
1 Put the fresh dulse into the boiling water and leave it to soak for as long as possible.

2 Blitz the cashew nuts in a food processor and then add the dried dulse and sugar and blend briefly.

3 Put the mixture into a dry shallow saucepan, and heat over low heat, stirring frequently, until it begins to brown.

4 Strain the dulse-infused water into a small jug and carefully add it to the browned sugar, cashews and dried dulse. Take care because the contents of the pan will be very hot. Stir well.

5 Cook over a low heat, until the mixture reduces to a golden nut and dulse syrup.

6 Turn onto an oiled sheet of foil and leave to set. Break into pieces and serve with ice cream.

Chocolate Sugar *Kelpmores*

Hebridean children once ate sugar kelp as candy (sweeties). Inspired by Hebridean history and the current craze for salted caramel, we came up with a sugar kelp winner. The idea of adding chocolate came from Estelle, a Greek medical student.

What to do:
1 Heat the sugar and chopped sugar kelp in a skillet (frying pan) over very low heat to melt the sugar slowly, and caramelize the sugar kelp. Stir occasionally with a wooden spoon. This will take about 45 minutes.

2 Leave the caramelized sugar kelp on a heatproof chopping board to cool completely.

3 Put the chocolate, butter, and dried sea lettuce in a small bowl that fits snugly over a pan of simmering water, to melt the butter and chocolate.

4 Add the caramelized sugar kelp, and stir gently to coat the kelp in the chocolate. Turn onto a piece of foil, and leave to dry completely. Store in an airtight container. This delicious snack is "moreish".

Makes about 2oz (55g)

What to forage and find:
* 3 tablespoons granulated sugar
* 4 tablespoons chopped dried sugar kelp (½–1-inch/1–2cm length)
* 1 square (25g) bittersweet (dark) chocolate (minimum 85% cocoa solids)
* 2 teaspoons (10g) unsalted butter
* Large pinch dried sea lettuce

Dulse PESTO

Use dulse pesto on pasta, pile on top of fish before baking, or add to cream or yogurt in sauces. Sea lettuce pesto can be made in the same way, and the color contrast of sea lettuce pesto on oven-baked salmon is simply stunning.

Makes 1 small bowl

What to forage and find:
* ½ cup (30g) grated Parmesan cheese
* 2 tablespoons dried dulse
* Scant ½ cup (50g) walnut halves
* Juice of 1 small lemon
* Approximately ⅓ cup (75ml) extra virgin olive oil
* Freshly ground black pepper (a few twists)

What to do:
1 Put all of the ingredients except the oil and pepper into a food processor, and blend well.

2 Add enough oil to make a thick paste, and add pepper to taste.

3 Put into a small bowl, cover, and refrigerate for up to 4–5 days, or freeze.

Try making a simple Dulse Tapenade, joining the darkness of tapenade with the taste of the sea. Use 1 clove garlic, ³/₄ cup (100g) chopped black olives, 2 tablespoons dried dulse, juice of 1 small lemon and enough olive oil to make a paste, whizzed in a food processor.

The dulse in this pesto can be replaced with washed and dried dandelion leaves for a delicious dandelion pesto. My son, Xavier, made this for lunch, mixing it with cream to make a sauce. He added sautéed dandelion buds (not flowers that have closed for the night), crispy bacon, and pasta—bravo, Son Number Four!

Wild Notes

Where I live on the Outer Hebrides, sheep and cows wander down to the beach, and eat seaweed, so adding a seaweed pesto mixed with breadcrumbs to coat a rack of lamb is a natural progression. Cooked on a beach barbecue, it's crunchy and delicious; cold leftovers are yummy served with a Seaweed Mayonnaise, page 135, or rowan jelly.

Away from the beach, the dulse can be replaced by ramps, to make Ramps (Wild Garlic) Pesto. This can be mixed with breadcrumbs and piled high on rowan jelly-glazed racks of lamb.

The addition of sea lettuce gives these traditionally rather weighty little cakes, immortalized by Proust, a seaside moistness that extends their shelf life and improves flavor after a day or so. We left some in a tin for well over a week, and they were still moist and delicious.

Sea Lettuce MADELEINES

Makes 24

What to forage and find:
* Flour and butter for Madeleine pans
* 1 level tablespoon of finely ground dried sea lettuce
* ⅔ cup (125g) superfine (caster) sugar
* 4 eggs
* 1 scant cup (125g) all-purpose (plain) flour, sifted
* 1 teaspoon baking powder
* 1 stick + 2 teaspoons (125g) butter, melted
* 1 tablespoon confectioners' (icing) sugar

What to do:
1 Preheat the oven to 425°F (220°C/gas mark 7).

2 Prepare the Madeleine pans by brushing them with melted butter, and lightly dusting with flour. Turn the pans upside down and shake out the excess flour. Set aside.

3 Blend the sea lettuce and sugar in a food processor. Blend briefly, so that the sea lettuce is well mixed into the sugar.

4 In a bowl, whisk the eggs, sea lettuce, and sugar together, until light and thick (the whisk leaves a trail in the bowl when lifted).

5 Fold in half of the sifted flour with the baking powder.

6 Drizzle half of the melted butter around the edge of the mixing bowl, and gently fold it in. When the ingredients have combined, repeat with the remaining flour and butter. Chill in the fridge for an hour. (This gives the mixture its dense, mousse-like consistency.)

7 Just over half-fill the prepared Madeleine pans (do not fill to the brim —they will expand during cooking), then bake for about 10 minutes, until the Madeleines are golden and speckled with sea lettuce green.

8 Give the pans a good shake to help remove the cakes. Turn onto a rack to cool. Dust with sifted confectioners' (icing) sugar.

Wild Notes
You might like to add a pinch of finely ground sea lettuce to the confectioners' (icing) sugar used to dust the cakes at Step 8. Alternatively, you can use sea lettuce sugar if you have made some.

Lemon and *Sea Lettuce* ICE CREAM

A velvety ice cream—just right for the beach.

Serves 4–6

What to forage and find:
* 3 unwaxed lemons
* 1 cup (200g) superfine (caster) sugar
* Scant 2 cups (450ml) light (single) cream
* 2 heaping teaspoons dried sea lettuce

What to do:

1 Finely grate the zest of one lemon and squeeze the juice from all three into a bowl and stir in the sugar.

2 Slowly add the cream and sea lettuce, mixing carefully—it will thicken.

3 Churn in an ice-cream maker and serve immediately.

If you do not have an ice cream maker, put the mixture into a freezer container, and freeze until slushy. Return the mixture to the bowl, beat well or whiz in a food processor, and return to the freezer. Repeat this process until you can't see any icy crystals, and then freeze until frozen. Allow the ice cream to soften slightly in a refrigerator before serving.

Sea Lettuce and Caramel Sauce

I was thinking about salted caramel on a Hebridean beach, the thought turned to seaweed and caramel sauce, and I made this delicious dish that very evening. I've made it with sea lettuce because I love the emerald specks dotted through the caramel, but you could use dried dulse or kelp if you prefer.

Makes 1¼ cups (300ml)

What to forage and find:
* ¾ cup (175ml) heavy (double) cream
* 2 heaping teaspoons dried and finely ground sea lettuce
* ⅔ cup (150ml) water
* 1½ cups (300g) superfine (caster) sugar

What to do:

1 Measure the cream into a measuring cup (jug), and add the dried sea lettuce. Stir and set aside.

2 Put the water in a heavy-based pan, and add the sugar. Try not to let the sugar touch the sides of the pan. I use a wide skillet (frying pan). Dissolve the sugar as slowly as possible over low heat.

3 Increase the heat and simmer until the sugar begins to caramelize—this will take 15–20 minutes. Stir occasionally.

4 When the sugar begins to brown, do not stir, but shake the pan to ensure an even heat distribution.

5 When the caramel is golden, remove the pan from the heat, and quickly add the prepared sea lettuce cream—stand back because the caramel will splutter. Stir vigorously to mix in the cream.

6 Cool for a few minutes, then pour into a pitcher (jug), and serve hot with ice cream or comfort desserts.

7 Alternatively, pour into a jam jar, cover when cold, and refrigerate for 4–5 days.

Scotch Quail Eggs with *Sea Lettuce*

These eggs are great finger food, delicious for picnics, and a good size for children.

What to do:

1 Hard-boil the quails' eggs in simmering water for 2½ minutes. Rinse the eggs in cold water, and peel the shells. I find this easier under running water; as with hens' eggs, some are easier to peel than others.

2 Put the sausage meat into a bowl and knead lightly.

3 Wrap each hard-boiled egg in sea lettuce, then dust your hands lightly with flour and take a small handful of sausage meat. Pack this around the sea-lettuce-wrapped egg, and gently mold the mixture to cover the egg.

4 Blend the bread in a food processor to make breadcrumbs, add the dried sea lettuce, blend briefly to mix, and put it into a small bowl.

5 Put the flour and lightly beaten egg into separate small bowls. Roll each quail egg in flour, egg (shake off any excess), and then sea lettuce breadcrumbs. Chill in a refrigerator for 20 minutes.

6 Follow the manufacturer's instructions to fill a deep fryer with oil, heat, and cook the Scotch eggs at 350°F (180°C) for 2½–3 minutes (depending on the thickness of the sausage meat), until golden. Cook the eggs in small batches. A slotted spoon is useful to remove the eggs from the deep fryer.

Makes 12

What to forage and find:
* 12 quails' eggs
* 13 oz (375g) pork sausage meat
* 12 x 2-inch (5cm) square pieces of fresh sea lettuce
* 2 slices of bread
* 1 tablespoon dried and ground sea lettuce
* 1 tablespoon all-purpose (plain) flour, plus extra for dusting
* 1 egg, lightly beaten

Lili's Fishy Fries

Sometimes the best recipes are created when cooking with friends, in this case my daughter Lili, Estelle, a visiting medical student, and a vegetarian friend, Charlotte. Lili decided to wrap potato wedges in sea lettuce, which retains its color during cooking, coat them in flour and egg, and then deep-fry. The result was sheer seaweedy deliciousness similar to fish'n'chips.

What to do:

1 Peel the potato and cut it into 6 wedges.

2 Put the flour and lightly beaten egg into 2 separate bowls.

3 Wrap each potato wedge in sea lettuce, coat it with flour, and then egg, and deep-fry at 350°F (180°C) for 5 minutes. Remove for a minute and then deep-fry again for an additional 1–2 minutes until golden. Cook in small batches, and do not allow the wedges to touch each other. Exact timing will depend on the potato wedge size, and the deep fryer model.

Makes 6 wedges

What to forage and find:
* 1 large potato
* All-purpose (plain) flour
* 1 lightly beaten egg
* 6 x 2-inch (5cm) square pieces fresh sea lettuce

Wild Notes

Serve with Sea Lettuce Mayonnaise, page 135. Charlotte, an Edinburgh University student, helped me test this recipe; she is vegetarian, and she coated some additional eggs in seaweed breadcrumbs without the sausage—it worked well. Charlotte also suggests cooking wild mushrooms in a similar coating.

Sea Lettuce fish parcels

I used sea kale in the Scottish round of *BBC Masterchef*, but on that occasion a local asparagus grower supplied my sea kale. Maxim, my fifth son, once spied sea kale while we were foraging; he wasn't sure what he'd found, and had to cope with an ecstatic shriek from his mother on its identification.

What to do:

1 Season the fish fillets with ground pepper and wrap each fillet in sea lettuce.

2 Pour the poaching liquid into a shallow pan and add the bay leaf and peppercorns. Bring the water to a boil, then simmer and carefully drop the parcels into the poaching liquid, using a slotted spoon. Pack the parcels tightly together to ensure that they keep their shape. Cover the pan with a lid, which will both poach and steam the fish.

3 Cook, covered, for 5–6 minutes until just done. Take the parcels out of the pan and remove the sea lettuce. Serve the fish with steamed sea kale (if in season) and *Sea Lettuce Butter Sauce* (below).

Serves 4

What to forage and find:
* 4 x 5 oz (150g) sustainable white fish fillets
* Freshly ground black pepper
* 4 pieces sea lettuce, 4 x 4 inches (10 x 10cm)
* Scant cup (200ml) poaching liquid (half white wine, half water)
* 1 bay leaf
* 2–3 peppercorns

Sea Lettuce butter sauce

An adaptation of my *BBC Masterchef* recipe.

What to forage and find:
* 1 shallot, finely chopped
* 3 tablespoons of rice vinegar
* 3 tablespoons water
* 2 sticks (225g) chilled sea lettuce butter, diced (see Seaweed Butter, page 148)
* 4 oz (110g) sea kale (6 pieces)

What to do:

1 Put the shallot, vinegar, and water into a skillet (frying pan). Heat until the liquid is reduced to 2 tablespoons.

2 Reduce the heat and slowly whisk in the sea lettuce butter, piece by piece. Season to taste.

3 Meanwhile, steam the sea kale for 3–4 minutes, and serve with the sea lettuce butter sauce and poached fish (*Sea Lettuce Fish Parcels*, above).

Wild Notes

In summer you might replace the sea kale with asparagus served in an elderflower vinegar and butter sauce.

Asparagus and Salmon wrapped in Sea Lettuce

These three simple ingredients, when combined together, are absolutely mouth-wateringly delicious.

Makes 8

What to forage and find:

* 8 asparagus spears (medium thickness), trimmed
* 8 pieces fresh sea lettuce, well washed
* 8 slices smoked salmon, approximately 7 oz (200g)

What to do:

1 Trim the asparagus to remove any woody stems, and blanch in boiling water for 30 seconds. Refresh in cold water and drain well.

2 Cut the sea lettuce to fit the smoked salmon slices roughly, and lay a slice of smoked salmon on a piece of sea lettuce.

3 Roll up the asparagus tip in the sea lettuce and salmon, as tightly as possible. About ½–¾ of the asparagus will be covered, leaving part of the stem uncovered.

4 Steam for 3–4 minutes (depending on size), and eat immediately, drizzled with lemon vinaigrette or a hollandaise sauce.

Sea & Shore

Sea Lettuce and Prawn PANNA COTTA

Panna cotta doesn't have to mean dessert. Its creamy texture is perfect with prawns, and infusing the cream with sea lettuce enhances its provenance.

What to do:

1 Put the sea lettuce and milk in a saucepan, and heat over very low heat for 20 minutes to reconstitute the sea lettuce, remove from the heat, and leave to infuse until cold.

2 Soak the gelatin sheets (leaves) in cold water for 3–4 minutes to soften.

3 Strain the seaweed-infused milk into a pan, retaining a teaspoon of sea lettuce. You should be left with a generous cupful (250ml) of milk. Put the strained milk and cream into a heavy-based saucepan. Bring to a boil slowly, and then remove from the heat.

4 Squeeze any excess water from the softened gelatin, and add the gelatin to the seaweed cream. Stir really well to dissolve the gelatin completely.

5 Pour the mixture into a pitcher (jug), and cool slightly.

6 Lightly oil the molds. Put a sprinkling of the reserved sea lettuce in the base of each mold, and add 8 shrimp (prawns) to each mold. Divide the sea lettuce panna cotta between the molds, and refrigerate until set.

7 Briefly dip the molds in warm water, and turn out onto individual plates.

8 Serve with a thin tomato sauce or chopped tomatoes.

Makes 6

What to forage and find:
* ✳ 2 teaspoons finely ground dried sea lettuce
* ✳ 1¼ cups (300ml) milk
* ✳ 3 sheets (leaves) gelatin (small)
* ✳ 1 generous cup (250ml) heavy (double) cream
* ✳ 24 cooked shrimp (prawns), about 10½ oz (300g)
* ✳ Thin tomato sauce or chopped tomatoes, to serve
* ✳ 4 x 3½fl oz (100ml) dariole molds or ramekins

Wild Notes

Try replacing the shrimp
with crabmeat, and for
a really wild set, use
carrageen instead of gelatin.

Sea Kelp MUFFINS

The addition of parchment paper cases adds a rustic touch to a common recipe with a totally original seaside taste.

What to do:

1 Preheat the oven to 375°F (190°C/gas mark 5).

2 Line each muffin cup with two squares of parchment paper arranged crosswise, so that four corners of parchment stand proud above the cup.

3 Put the flour, baking powder, sugar, and dried sea lettuce into a mixing bowl.

4 Measure the milk and oil into a large measuring cup, and whisk together. Add the egg and mix well.

5 Add the Chocolate Sugar Kelpmores to the dry ingredients and then quickly fold the liquid in, so that the mixture is just mixed.

6 Use a tablespoon to spoon the mixture into the lined muffin cups.

7 Bake in the oven for 20–25 minutes until golden.

8 Remove the muffins from the oven, and transfer the hot muffins to a cooling rack.

Makes 12

What to forage and find:
* ✳ 24 x 5-inch (12cm) squares parchment paper
* ✳ 2¼ cups (300g) self-rising flour
* ✳ 1 teaspoon baking powder
* ✳ ½ cup (100g) superfine (caster) sugar
* ✳ 1 heaping teaspoon finely ground dried sea lettuce
* ✳ ¾ cup (175ml) milk
* ✳ Generous ½ cup (125ml) vegetable oil
* ✳ 1 egg
* ✳ ⅓ cup (50g) *Chocolate Sugar Kelpmores*, page 160 (larger ones crushed)

Sugar Kelp CRISPS

Sugar kelp was once sold in the streets as a snack, so these crisps seem appropriate.

Make as many as you like (4–6 crisps per portion)

What to forage and find:
* ✳ Fresh sugar kelp
* ✳ Vegetable oil

What to do:

1 Use scissors to cut the sea kelp into pieces. Mine were about 3 x 2 inches (8 x 5cm), but you may prefer larger or smaller sugar kelp crisps.

2 Follow the manufacturer's instructions to fill a deep fryer with oil. Heat the oil to 350°F (180°C) and cook the crisps for a minute or so, depending on thickness.

3 Use with wild dips, or simply savor the seaweed flavor on its own. You may prefer to brush the pieces of sugar kelp with oil and bake the crisps in a moderate oven for 10–15 minutes, depending on thickness.

Wild Mint and Carrageen BLANCMANGE

I tend to use more carrageen than most recipes suggest—2 handfuls (20g) to set 1¼ cups (300ml) of liquid. But in this recipe, the milk and cream help the set, so that not as much is required. Some of the old Hebridean recipes that I have come across seem to be the consistency of a jelly drink.

Serves 6

What to forage and find:
* 1 handful (10g) dried carrageen
* 2½ cups (600ml) milk
* Sprig of wild mint
* ⅔ cup (150ml) heavy (double) cream
* 4 teaspoons wild mint sugar, if available. (Otherwise, just use superfine [caster] sugar)
* 1 teaspoon chopped wild mint leaves

What to do:
1 Rinse the carrageen well and leave it to soak for 20 minutes.

2 Heat the milk, well-squeezed carrageen, and mint in a heavy-based saucepan. Simmer over low heat for 30 minutes, until the mixture thickens and becomes gelatinous.

3 Push the mixture through a sieve into a pitcher (jug), squeezing as much liquid through as possible, to push the natural gelatin through.

4 Return the liquid to the pan, and add the cream and sugar to taste. Cook briefly for 1–2 minutes and add the chopped mint leaves.

5 Pour into a prepared mold (or individual molds), and leave to cool completely. Refrigerate until set. Turn the blancmange out on a serving dish.

Pickled Dulse

You may prefer to use sugar kelp in place of dulse. Pickled seaweed can be added to mayonnaise.

Makes 1 small jar

What to forage and find:
* Dried dulse
* ½ small clove garlic, bruised
* Approximately 1 cup (250ml) cider vinegar
* Pinch of mustard seeds
* 1 teaspoon superfine (caster) sugar
* 2–3 black peppercorns

What to do:
1 Rehydrate the dulse and cut into 1½ x ¼ inch (4cm x 5mm) lengths (about 5–6 tablespoons total), and tightly pack them into a small jam jar. Add the garlic.

2 Heat the remaining ingredients in a saucepan and bring to a boil briefly. Pour the vinegar and spices over the dulse and allow to cool.

3 Seal with a vinegar-proof lid, and store for 1 month to allow the flavors to infuse.

Pickling Note

Use stainless steel utensils, glass jars, and nylon sieves, because the acid in vinegar can react with the metal and cause the pickled ingredients to taste bitter. Sterilize jam jars in a dishwasher, or wash them in hot soapy water, then dry them in a low oven 300°F (150°C/gas 2).

Sea & Shore

The orange butternut squash and vibrant green fleck of the sea lettuce in the coating contrast vividly with each other, and add elegance to a frugal supper or lunch dish.

Seaweed and BUTTERNUT SQUASH Cakes

Makes 6

What to forage and find:
* Fresh dulse, about 3¼ inches (8cm)
* 2½ cups (350g) peeled, seeded, and diced raw butternut squash
* 2 teaspoons vegetable oil
* 1 tablespoon (15g) butter
* 4 teaspoons dried dulse
* 18 oz (500g) potatoes (good mashing variety)
* 1 tablespoon chopped almonds
* 2 slices bread
* 1 handful (heaping tablespoon) dried sea lettuce
* 2 tablespoons all-purpose (plain) flour, plus extra for dusting
* 1 egg, lightly beaten
* Oil and butter for cooking

What to do:

1 Preheat the oven to 350°F (180°C/gas mark 4).

2 Put the fresh dulse in a saucepan half full of boiling water and set aside

3 Put the squash on a baking pan (tin), and drizzle the oil and dot the butter over the top. Sprinkle the dried dulse over, then cover with foil and bake for 30–35 minutes until the squash is tender.

4 Meanwhile, peel the potatoes and dice into even-sized chunks. Put the potatoes into the pan of water with the dulse and bring to a boil. Simmer for 10–12 minutes, or until the potatoes are just soft. Drain well and discard the dulse.

5 In a bowl, mash the roasted butternut squash, potatoes, and almonds together, and leave to cool.

6 Divide the mixture into 6, form into cakes, and put them on a tray. Refrigerate for an hour.

7 In a food processor, blend the bread to make breadcrumbs, and add the sea lettuce. Put the breadcrumb mixture in a shallow bowl, the flour in a second bowl, and the lightly beaten egg in a third bowl.

8 Flour your hands, and dip the seaweed and squash cakes in the flour, then the egg wash, and then coat in the seaweed breadcrumbs. Refrigerate the cakes for at least 30 minutes.

9 Heat a tablespoon of oil and a knob of butter in a frying pan, and cook the cakes for 4–5 minutes on each side until golden brown, replenishing the butter and oil as necessary.

Wild Notes

Delicious served with Common
Sorrel Sauce, page 87, or
Nettle Purée, page 64.

Beach POPCORN

Credit for this fun recipe goes to my daughter Lili and her student friends. It has to be top of the snack list for a beach party.

Serves 4

What to forage and find:
* ¼ cup (50g) unpopped popcorn kernels
* 2 scant tablespoons (25g) *Seaweed Butter*, page 148
* Zest and juice of ½ lime
* Heaping teaspoon of finely ground sea lettuce

What to do:

1 Either pop your own corn on the stovetop (hob) following the manufacturer's instructions, or cook it in the microwave.

2 Meanwhile, melt the seaweed butter in a saucepan, ensuring that it doesn't brown, and add the finely grated lime zest and juice.

3 Turn the hot popcorn into a bowl, and pour over the seaweed butter and lime. Toss well, then add the sea lettuce. Mix again briefly, and eat as soon as possible.

Chocolate Beach POPCORN

A variation for chocoholics on the beach!

Serves 4

What to forage and find:
* ¼ cup (50g) unpopped popcorn kernels
* 3 tablespoons + 1 teaspoon (50g) unsalted butter
* 1 heaping teaspoon dried dulse or kelp, or less, to taste
* 1 oz (25g) white chocolate
* 1 square (25g) bittersweet (dark) chocolate (minimum 85% cocoa solids)

What to do:

1 Either pop your own corn on the stovetop (hob) following the manufacturer's instructions, or cook it in the microwave.

2 Divide the butter and seaweed between two bowls. Add white chocolate to one and bittersweet (dark) chocolate to the other.

3 Heat the bowls of butter and chocolate in a microwave, or over a pan of simmering water until melted. Stir well.

4 Divide the popcorn into two bowls and pour the melted white seaweed chocolate into one bowl, and the dark seaweed chocolate into the other. Toss to coat and, when set, combine the two for delicious salty chocolate popcorn.

River and Sea RICE Supper

This is a simple lunch or supper dish. It is really a question of ensuring that everything is cooking simultaneously and then assembling the cooked ingredients together.

Serves 6

What to forage and find:
* 1¾ cups (300g) long-grain rice
* 2 teaspoons dried sea lettuce
* 4 x 7oz (200g) salmon trout (sea trout) fillets
* 2-inch (5cm) piece of fresh sea lettuce
* 12 quails' eggs
* ¾ cup (100g) frozen small peas (petit pois)
* Scant 2 tablespoons (25g) sea lettuce butter, melted (see *Seaweed Butter*, page 148)
* Freshly ground black pepper
* 1 teaspoon finely chopped sea lettuce

What to do:

1 Rinse the rice, and cook as directed on the package, adding 2 teaspoons dried sea lettuce to the water. Drain well, and rinse with boiling water. Cover with foil, and keep warm.

2 Put the trout in a pan. Add just enough water to cover and a 2-inch (5cm) piece of fresh sea lettuce.* Bring the water to a boil, and poach for 2 minutes, or until the fillets are cooked. Remove and roughly flake the fish. Add it to the rice.

3 Meanwhile, hard-boil the eggs (about 2½ minutes). Drain, and put the eggs in ice water. Allow the eggs to cool, and peel off the shells. Cut the eggs in half lengthwise, and put them in the serving dish.

4 Cook the peas in boiling water for 1–2 minutes, and drain. Add the peas to the rice and eggs.

5 Drizzle the melted sea lettuce butter over the cooked ingredients, season with ground pepper and a teaspoonful of finely chopped sea lettuce.

*Alternatively, you can steam the fish, or if you don't have fresh sea lettuce, use a teaspoonful of dried seaweed.

Wild Notes

Lightly roll hard-boiled quails' eggs in finely ground dried sea lettuce (or homemade sea lettuce salt), and serve as a canapé. I like to leave an unpeeled quail egg on the serving dish; the shells are so pretty.

You could use Pickled Quail Eggs, page 35, as canapés, too, or use pickled eggs in this recipe for added punch. A pinch of dried sea lettuce, kelp, or dulse is also delicious in scrambled eggs, or sprinkled over a speckled hen's egg for breakfast.

Razor clams are the ultimate forager's delight: they are a tease to catch and, once caught, pop in and out of the shell in a rather rude and disturbing manner. There will be a lot of live action in the bucket in which you collect your spoils. I make no excuse for the simplicity of this recipe; the time and excitement spent foraging is complicated enough. In my opinion, cooking should take place as soon as possible, and as close to where the clams were foraged as possible. However, some people prefer to leave the clams to soak overnight to remove grit and sand.

Simply *Razor Clams*

Serves 4

What to forage and find:
* 20 razor clams, cleaned
* 4½ oz (125g) garlic butter
* 2 tablespoons roughly chopped parsley
* Crusty bread, to serve

What to do:

1 Half-fill a large, shallow pan with water and bring it to a boil. Add the razor clams and cover with a tightly fitting lid.

2 Bring the pan back to a boil and simmer for a minute, or until the razor clams open. Use a slotted spoon to remove the clams from the pan. Do not overcook them or they will become tough.

3 When the razor clams are cool enough to handle, remove the clam flesh from the shells (I use my hands). Discard any shells that haven't opened.

4 Cut the razor clams into pieces if you like, I tend to serve them whole; 4–5 razor clams per person is a generous portion.

5 Meanwhile, melt the garlic butter, add the parsley, and pour it over the hot razor clams. Eat immediately, with hot crusty bread to mop up the juices.

Wild Notes

Razor clams look spectacular served in their shells. Chargrilled chorizo or bacon works well with them, as do other ingredients used in scallop recipes. Razor clams can also be used in chowder.

At the beach, barbecue the razor clams (or cook in the hot fire embers) until they open and then cook briefly, flesh side down, on the barbecue.

In spring, this substantial soup can be made with foraged watercress. It is warming on a cold spring day, when wild watercress is growing but an icy wind is blowing. Purists will use undyed haddock, but I love the dyed yellow color contrast with the vibrant wild green of the watercress and cooked dulse.

Smoked Haddock, Dulse, and Watercress Soup

What to do:

1 Over low heat, melt the butter and oil in a saucepan. Add the onion, and cook briefly, then add the diced potatoes, dried dulse, and oats. Stir well to coat the potatoes in oil, cover, and simmer over very low heat for 5 minutes. Stir occasionally, to check that the potatoes aren't sticking to the pan. Add a little milk if necessary.

2 Add the milk and the haddock, skin-side up. Cover and continue cooking over low heat.

3 After about 4–5 minutes (when the fish has poached) lift the haddock out of the liquid with a fish slice and remove the skin. Gently flake the fish, keeping the chunks as large as possible, and return them to the pan. Add the water and watercress, and continue to cook for 2–3 minutes. Use a knife to test that the potato is cooked, and serve immediately.

Serves 4

What to forage and find:
* ¼ stick (30g) butter
* 1 tablespoon olive oil
* 1 onion, peeled and chopped
* 9 oz (250g) potatoes, peeled and diced small
* 1 tablespoon roughly chopped dried dulse
* 1 tablespoon steel-cut oats (pinhead oatmeal)
* 2 generous cups (500ml) milk
* 7oz (200g) smoked haddock fillet
* About 1¼ cups (300ml) water
* 2 tablespoons roughly chopped watercress

Wild Notes
For a splash of emerald color, sprinkle with finely ground sea lettuce before serving.

Samphire (glasswort) is delicious on its own or served in hot or cold sauces with fish. This recipe works just as well with salmon.

Samphire with Plaice in Sweet Pepper Sauce

What to do:

1 Cut the peppers in half lengthwise, remove the seeds, and put them skin side up on a baking sheet under a pre-heated broiler (grill). When the skins have charred, remove them from the pan, and put them in a plastic bag. Allow some air to remain in the bag, and loosely tie it. The steam in the bag will help to remove the skins. When cool enough to handle, peel off the skins. Put the peppers into a food processor and blend to a purée.

2 Fill a wide, shallow pan with water (just enough to cover the plaice fillets). Add the slices of lime and bring the water to a boil. When the water is just at the point of simmering, add the plaice fillets, cover with a lid, and remove the pan from the heat. The fish will poach in the cooling water (5 minutes). Keep the fish warm.

3 Turn the pepper purée into a saucepan, and add 2–3 tablespoons of the strained poaching stock to make a pouring sauce. Heat through and season with freshly ground pepper.

4 Trim the samphire, removing any woody stems, and rinse it well under running water. Drain, and pat dry. Cook the samphire very briefly (30 seconds) in a pan of boiling water. Drain and refresh in cold water–this will bring out its color without loss of flavor.

5 Heat the butter in a pan and sauté the chili and ginger briefly. Add the samphire and cook for 2–3 minutes in the spiced butter.

6 Divide the warm samphire between four plates. Add a fish fillet to each plate, and spoon on the pepper sauce in equal portions. You might like to serve *Lili's Fishy Fries*, page 166, with this recipe, instead of the fish.

Serves 4

What to forage and find:
* 2 Ramiro peppers (elongated red sweet peppers)
* 4 x 3½ oz (100g) plaice fillets
* 1 small lime, thinly sliced
* 10½ oz (300g) samphire (8–10 large handfuls)
* 2 tablespoons (25g) (or ¼ stick) butter
* ½ green chili, deseeded and finely diced
* ½ teaspoon finely chopped fresh ginger
* Freshly ground black pepper

Wild Notes

Try making a salad adaptation of this recipe, using stir-fried samphire and hot smoked salmon. Samphire has a natural affinity with fish; you often spy it on fishmongers' displays (one way to identify it before you forage) but it also works well with lamb. Samphire can also be enjoyed in a sea-lettuce infused tempura batter.

Sea & Shore

When I asked my husband Stephen to try to find heather ale on the Hebridean Isle of South Uist, I thought it "mission impossible". In the event, he returned with a bottle of dandelion and burdock beer, which seemed appropriate for this recipe, albeit not technically foraged by me.

Wild Mussels in Dandelion and Burdock Beer

What to do:

1 Put the diced onion, ramps stalks, and dandelion and burdock beer into a large saucepan and bring to a boil. Simmer to reduce slightly, and to soften the onion. Add the clean mussels, and cover with a lid.

2 Simmer gently for 3–4 minutes, shaking the pan from time to time, until the shells open.

3 Remove the mussels (discarding any shells that have not opened). Add the segmented ramp flowers. Heat briefly and serve immediately with crusty bread *Lili's Fishy Fries*, page 166.

Serves 2–3

What to forage and find:
* Small red onion, peeled and diced
* 1 tablespoon chopped ramps (wild garlic) stalks (or 1 clove garlic)
* Generous 1½ cups (275ml) dandelion and burdock beer, or root beer
* About 3¼ lb (1.5kg) mussels, cleaned and beards removed
* 2 ramps (wild garlic) flowers, segmented (seasonal option)

Wild Notes

For a richer version, add ⅔ cup (150ml) cream at Step 3.

Half fill a large shallow pan with seaweed and seawater and pop the mussels on top of the seaweed. Cover the pan with foil and put it on a hot barbecue. Check after 5 minutes to see if any mussels have opened (cooked). Species of wrack, which grow on the upper shore, are an easy seaweed to forage and use on a beach barbeque.

Foraging and the Law

Foragers need to take personal responsibility and add a huge "pinch" of common sense to their cooking pot. As a forager, you need to understand the law, by-laws, and tides, and learn about the ingredients for yourself; there isn't a short cut. With foraging comes an understanding of your local land, but a bountiful harvest cannot be guaranteed from year to year; this is the forager's challenge Yes, ask others for advice (or go on a course), but a forager's knowledge grows with experience; it isn't something that can be spoon-fed. If you want wild ingredients without effort, buy them from a commercial forager, but in so doing, you lose the joy of the foraging process; even if it might involve doffing your cap to a landowner, or returning home, cold and wet, with an empty basket. Do not forage any roots without the landowner's permission—even invasive species.

Laws differ from country to country so please check local regulations before you start. The following websites may be useful:

UK (not Scotland)
www.legislation.gov.uk/ukpga/1968/60/contents

Theft act 1968
"A person who picks mushrooms growing wild on any land, or who picks flowers, fruit or foliage from a plant growing wild on any land, does not (although not in possession of the land) steal what he picks, unless he does it for reward, or for sale, or other commercial purpose."

Be aware of by-laws, which, in places, may remove foraging rights.

National Parks and Access to The Countryside Act 1949
www.legislation.gov.uk/ukpga/Geo6/12-13-14/97

The Countryside and Rights Of Way Act 2000 (CROW)
www.legislation.gov.uk/ukpga/2000/37/contents

Joint Nature Conservation Committee
http://jncc.defra.gov.uk/page-1377
(The Wildlife and Countryside Act 1981)

The Countryside Code
www.naturalengland.org.uk/ourwork/enjoying/countrysidecode/default.aspx

National Parks (protected areas)
www.naturalengland.org.uk/ourwork/conservation/designatedareas/nationalparks/default.aspx

Sites of Special Scientific Interest :
Foraging here is illegal, although it is unlikely that you will be prosecuted for foraging common ingredients such as blackberries, but protected species, yes.
www.defra.gov.uk/rural/protected/nationally/sssi/

Marine:
Sea Fish (Conservation) Act 1967
www.legislation.gov.uk/ukpga/1967/84
www.legislation.gov.uk/uksi/2012/827/made

Ownership and sustainable seaweed harvesting in Northern Ireland
www.doeni.gov.uk/niea/seaweedharvestingniehsposition statement.pdf

Marine Conservation Society
www.mcsuk.org/

Useful Local Links
www.association-ifca.org.uk/useful-links.html

Marine protected Areas
www.naturalengland.org.uk/our work/conservation/designatedar eas/mpa/default.aspx

Helpful websites UK:
The Linnean Society
www.linnean.org

Royal Forestry Society
www.rfs.org.uk/

Parish Maps
www.england-in-particular.info/cg/parishmaps/m-index.html

National Association for Environmental Education (UK)
www.nationalrural.org/organisation.aspx?id=caeafb14-5 fac-42a0-9904-05cd911eb257

Ramblers Association
www.ramblers.org.uk/freedom/Freedom+Sub+Home+Page (Access)
www.wildmanwildfood.com/pages/foraging%20and%20the%20law.htm (Law)

Foraging app
https://itunes.apple.com/gb/app/wild-food-forager/id394216031?mt=8

Scotland
The Land Reform Act 2003 gives Scots the right to be on most land and inland water providing they act responsibly and follow the terms of the Scottish Outdoor Access Code.

Scottish Natural Heritage
www.snh.gov.uk/protecting-scotlands-nature/protected-areas/national-designations/sssis
www.snh.gov.uk/protecting-scotlands-nature

Picking wild berries and fungi
www.outdooraccess-scotland.com/out-and-about/recreation-activities/berries-and-mushrooms

The Scottish Wild Mushroom Code:
www.forestharvest.org.uk/guidelines/Mushcode.htm

Ireland
www.forageireland.com/

Wales
www.visitwales.co.uk/about-wales-guide-to-wales-culture-people-and-language/food/foraging

US
US laws vary from state to state, and foragers in Texas should pay particular attention to state laws. A quirky leftover of a 19th- century law is that in Texas, people are not allowed to "graze" or gather food on public land. However, many Texas foragers gather with permission on the land of friends or neighbors. I'm told that the website, Bushcraft USA is particularly useful to foragers in the US.
http://bushcraftusa.com

National Aquaculture Act of 1980
http://www.nmfs.noaa.gov/sfa/sfweb/aqua_act.htm

United States Environmental Protection Agency Policy and Guidance
http://www.epa.gov/lawsregs/policy/

Wetlands Protection:
http://water.epa.gov/type/wetlands/protection.cfm

US Foraging Law:
http://definitions.uslegal.com/f/foraging-area/
North American Association for Environmental Education
http://www.naaee.net/

Invasive species:
www.invasive.org/species/weeds.cfm

Useful websites USA:
Mushroom picking:
www.somamushrooms.org

Maine Mushroom foraging (commercial)
http://mushroom-collecting.com

John Kallas Wild Food Adventures
http://wildfoodadventures.com/

Urban Edibles
http://urbanedibles.org/

Texas Foraging
www.foragingtexas.com/

Canada

www.gov.mb.ca/conservation/firstnations/hunting_fishing_oct_09.pdf

The Natural Resources Transfer Agreement (NRTA), which forms part of the Constitution Act, 1930, provides that Indian people "have the right, which the Province hereby assures to them, of hunting, trapping and fishing game and fish for food at all seasons of the year on all unoccupied Crown lands and on any other lands to which (they) may have a right of access." Treaty and Aboriginal rights relating to hunting, fishing and gathering are also recognized and affirmed as part of the Constitution of Canada by Section 35 of the Constitution Act, 1982.

Useful Canadian websites
http://northernbushcraft.com/index.htm
Invasive Species:
Canada : http://www.ec.gc.ca/eee-ias/default.asp?lang=En&n=1A81B051-1

Recommended Reading

Beeton I.: *Mrs Beeton's Book of Household Management*
Bissell, Frances: *The Scented Kitchen: Cooking with Flowers*
Britton, Nathaniel Lord: *Manual of the Flora of the Northern States and Canada*
Burrows, Ian: *Food From The Wild*
Duff, Gail (illustrated by Linda Garland): *The Countryside Cook Book: Recipes and Remedies*
Ellis, Lesley: *Simply Seaweed*
Grieve M. Mrs Edited and introduced by Leyel C.F. Mrs: *A Modern Herbal*

Grigson, Geoffrey: *The Englishman's Flora*
Hartley, Dorothy: *Food in England*
Hatfield, Gabrielle: *Encyclopedia of Folk Medicine: Old World and New World Traditions*
Irving, Miles: *The Forager Handbook*
Lewis-Stempel, John: *Foraging: The Essential Guide to Free Wild Food*
Leyel C.F. Mrs and Hartley, Olga Miss: *The Gentle Art of Cookery*
Mabey, Richard: *Flora Britannica The definitive new guide to wild flowers, plants, and trees; Food For Free; Wild Cooking*
Mabey, Richard: *Food for Free*

Mears, Ray: *Wild Food*
Michael, Pamela: *Edible Wild Plants and Herbs, a Compendium of Recipes and Remedies*
Michael, Pamela: *A Country Harvest*
Raven, Sarah: *Wild Flowers*
Rhatigan, Prannie: *Prannie Rhatigan's Irish Seaweed Kitchen*
White, Florence: *Flowers as Food*
Wright, John: *River Cottage Handbook No. 5: Edible Seashore*

Acknowledgments
For inspiration:
Fergus Drennan:
www.wildmanwildfood.co.uk
Flora Celtica:
http://193.62.154.38/celtica/fcb.htm
www.ediblemanhattan.com
Charlie Lee Potter http://eggsontheroof.com
Mark Williams (foraging courses)
www.gallowaywildfoods.com
www.thelivingweb.net/free_food_wild_food
www.wildgourmetfood.com/index.html
Steve Brill: www.wildmanstevebrill.com/

Seaweed support team: Prof Ian Rowland and Dr Sarah Hotchkiss University of Reading; Sarah MacLean of the Hebridean Isle of Barra.

My gratitude to:
Cindy Richards of Cico Books for the most amazing opportunity to write this book. Gillian Haslam of Cico Books for didactic guidance, at times separating the wood from the trees and encouraging me all along the way. Lee Faber for supportive editing and a "treasure box" email. Stuart West, Louise Wagstaffe, and Luis Peral Aranda for the recipe photography, and Alison Fenton for the book design.

For seaweed recipe development in the Hebridean kitchen: Lili Bird, Charlotte Kendal Parker, Estelle D'Cunha, and www.magimix.com
For pontack recipe testing:
www.audreygillan.com

Hebridean foragers: Jhonti, Xavier, and Maxim Bird
Angus foragers: Xander and Alasdair Bird
Faithful wild food taster: Rosemary Bird
Wild photographer: Pete Moore

For countryside memories: My grandparents, parents John and Joy Murray, my sister, Nicki and brother, Blair

And last but not least, my guinea pig and best friend, the doctor for the Hebridean Isle of South Uist, Stephen Bird. I will forever be indebted to you, not least for eating a month of seaweed suppers, and breakfasting on porridge with numerous wild syrups and seeds.

Recommended Reading

189

Index

Photographic credits

Recipe photos by Stuart West.
Foraging photos by Peter Moore,
apart from the following:
Page 6 Caroline Hughes
Page 12 Claire Richardson
Page 30 Claire Richardson
Page 56 David Merewether
Page 58 © Doug Sokell/Visuals Unlimited/
   Corbis
Page 68 © Laurence Mouton and Isabelle
   Rozenbaum/PhotoAlto/Corbis
Page 69 Lucinda Symons
Page 70 © Roger Wilmshurst/Frank Lane
   Picture Agency/Corbis
Page 73 David Merewether
Page 75 © Gary Cook/Visuals Unlimited/
   Corbis
Page 76 (top) © Jacqui Hurst/Corbis

Page 76 (center) © George McCarthy/Corbis
Page 91 Tara Fisher
Page 92 David Merewether
Page 94 David Merewether
Page 108 © FoodPhotography Eising/
   the food passionates/Corbis
Page 111 Gloria Nicol
Page 113 Gloria Nicol
Page 114 Gloria Nicol
Page 115 Gloria Nicol
Page 118 © Klaus Hackenberg/Corbis
Page 119 © Klaus Hackenberg/Corbis
Page 120 © Ocean/Corbis
Page 121 © Roger Tidman/Corbis
Page 125 David Merewether
Page 146 © Carol Sharp/http://www.
   flowerphotos.com/Eye Ubiquitous/Corbis
Page 151 © Radius Images/Corbis

Page 153 (center) © Niall Benvie/Corbis
Page 154 (bottom) © Ocean/Corbis
Page 155 (top right) © Jacqui Hurst/Corbis
Page 155 (bottom right) © Chinch
   Gryniewicz; Ecoscene/Corbis
Page 156 (top) © Carol Sharp/
   http://www.flowerphotos.com/
   Eye Ubiquitous/Corbis
Page 159 (top) © David Nunuk/All Canada
   Photos/Corbis
Page 159 (center) © Owen Franken/Corbis
Page 181 © Lemonnier, Nicolas/the food
   passionates/Corbis
Page 182 © Greg Rannels Photography
   Inc./the food passionates/Corbis
Page 185 © Jacqui Hurst/Corbis

Photographic Credits